100 WALKS IN
WILTSHIRE

THE CROWOOD PRESS

First published in 2015 by
The Crowood Press Ltd
Ramsbury, Marlborough
Wiltshire SN8 2HR

enquiries@crowood.com

www.crowood.com

This impression 2021

British Library Cataloguing-in-Publication Data
A catalogue record for this book is available from the British Library.

ISBN 978 1 78500 043 0

Mapping in this book is sourced from the following products: OS Explorer 118, 130, 131,
142, 143, 155, 156, 157, 158, 168, 169, 170
© Crown copyright Ordnance Survey. Licence number 100038003

Graphic design and layout by Peggy Issenman, www.peggyandco.ca
Printed and bound in India by Replika Press Pvt. Ltd.

Contents

How to Use this Book

The walks have been written in distance order, starting with the shortest at 2¼ miles and ending with the longest at 12 miles.

Readers should be aware that starting point postcodes have been supplied for satnav purposes and are not necessarily indicative of exact locations.

MAPS

There are 86 maps covering the 100 walks. Some of the walks are extensions of existing routes and the information panel for these walks will tell you the distance of the short and long versions of the walk. For those not wishing to undertake the longer versions of these walks, the 'short-cuts' are shown on the map in red.

The routes marked on the maps are punctuated by a series of numbered waypoints. These relate to the same numbers shown in the walk description.

Start Points

The start of each walk is given as a postcode and also a six-figure grid reference number prefixed by two letters (which indicates the relevant square on the National Grid). More information on grid references is found on Ordnance Survey maps.

Parking

Many of the car parks suggested are public, but for some walks you will have to park on the roadside or in a lay-by. Please be considerate when leaving your car and do not block access roads or gates. Also, if parking in a pub car park for the duration of the walk, please try to avoid busy times.

COUNTRYSIDE CODE
- Consider the local community and other people enjoying the outdoors
- Leave gates and property as you find them and follow paths
- Leave no trace of your visit and take litter home
- Keep dogs under effective control
- Plan ahead and be prepared
- Follow advice and local signs

Walks Locator

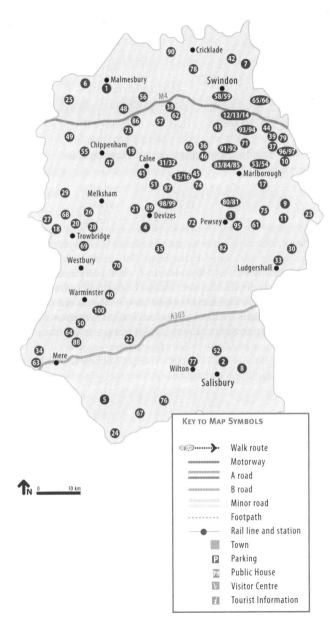

KEY TO MAP SYMBOLS

	Walk route
	Motorway
	A road
	B road
	Minor road
	Footpath
	Rail line and station
	Town
P	Parking
PH	Public House
V	Visitor Centre
i	Tourist Information

Malmesbury

START Station Yard (long stay car park), Malmesbury SN16 9JT, GR ST931875

DISTANCE 2¼ miles (3.5km)

SUMMARY Urban walk

MAPS OS Landranger 173 Swindon & Devizes; OS Explorer 168 Stroud, Tetbury & Malmesbury

WHERE TO EAT AND DRINK
Numerous places in Malmesbury

A gentle stroll along the picturesque streets and water meadows of England's oldest borough.

① Cross the river by the bridge at the end of the car park and go up the steps in front of you, bearing left as soon as you begin to climb. The steps lead to the remarkable Abbey House Gardens and Malmesbury Abbey, which you will want to explore in detail. Equally interesting is the picturesque wisteria-clad hotel called The Old Bell beside the Abbey. Leave the Abbey through the south door and go towards the Tolsey, or gatehouse, directly in front of you. Halfway along to the left of the path you may wish to search for the intriguing gravestone to the memory of Hannah Twynnoy. Go through the Tolsey and, passing the old Market Cross, cross Oxford St and head down the High St, bearing left downhill into Lower High St, from where a fine view of the Almshouses can be appreciated.

② Join the pavement on the right of the road and just before St John's Bridge go through a gateway on the right and then turn left over a footbridge above the Avon. As you cross the footbridge, you will see the town's silk mills, now converted into flats, to your left. Walk a few yards along the road before turning right through a gate into the watermeadow. Keeping the river on your right, proceed along the path for about half a mile, then cross a stone footbridge over a small stream. Turn to the right and go through a squeeze stile and along an embankment, then over a second and larger footbridge to the left.

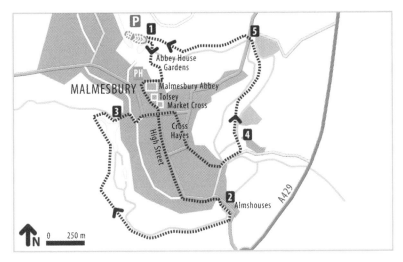

3 Go along the path between two stone walls then turn right up the sloping path marked 'Burnivale'. Turn left up the stone steps and follow the path to reach Gloucester St. Turn right to return to the Market Cross, then go straight on along Oxford St and turn right into Market La to reach Cross Hayes. Take the road in the opposite corner of the square. This is Silver St, so called because it once contained Malmesbury's mint. After a few yards the road gives way to gentle steps, until you reach the bottom of the hill, whereupon you turn left over the bridge and past the bowling green. At the edge of the green, turn left again, down a gravel footpath. This will take you first over a sluice-cum-footbridge and then over a stile into watermeadows.

4 After a further hundred yards or so, by an old derelict railway line, you will come to another stile. Go over this, keeping between the two courses of the River Avon (the Tetbury branch is alternatively known as the River Ingleburn). Eventually you reach a stile by a road going over a bridge.

5 Cross the road and take the path immediately in front of the pub car park. Continue along this path, with the river on your left, through the Conygre Mead Nature Reserve to return to the car park.

Points of interest

Malmesbury claims to be the oldest borough in England, having been granted a charter by Alfred the Great in 880. King Ethelstan, who is buried in the Abbey, later gave land to the town after its menfolk had helped him defeat Norse invaders. This land is still known as King's Heath. Virtually every building in Malmesbury has its own points of interest and is worth a moment of your time. Here we consider only those that, in the opinion of the author, are quite outstanding.

Abbey House: This fine building was erected in the sixteenth century after William Stumpe had bought the Abbey and its lands after the Dissolution of the Monasteries in the time of Henry VIII. He paid only £1,516 for the entire Abbey property. William Stumpe was a wealthy local clothier who set up his factory inside the Abbey itself, though two years later he gave the nave to the town for use as a church. Abbey House Gardens have been developed since 1994 and are open 11am–5.30pm daily 21 Mar–end Oct.

Malmesbury Abbey: The first abbey was founded by St Aldhelm in the seventh century, though what we now see was mainly built in the twelfth century. Restoration work was carried out in the fourteenth century when a mighty tower was added, standing some 445ft high. This collapsed in the fifteenth century, destroying much of the eastern end of the church, but nevertheless the abbey is still one of the finest examples of Norman ecclesiastical architecture anywhere in the country. Notice particularly the magnificent twelfth-century carved porch, the tomb of King Ethelstan, the first Saxon king to rule the whole of England, who died in 940, and the mysterious little watching loft on the south wall. When the Parvise is open, some fascinating manuscripts, coins and documents are on view. In the eleventh century a monk at the Abbey, one Elmer, jumped off the tower wearing home-made wings in the vain belief that he had discovered the secret of man-powered flight. One story has him gliding over 200yds before he crashed. He broke both his legs and was crippled for the rest of his life. Elmer's flight is today commemorated in a stained-glass window.

The Old Bell: It is believed that the inn may well have once been part of a Saxon castle which is known to have been demolished in 1216. Since the site was then used for the Abbey guesthouse, part of the inn's walls are thought to be from that building.

Tolsey: This gatehouse guards the entrance to the Abbey grounds and was possibly the town lock-up. The Apostle's Spoon, on the left as you leave the Abbey, is the oldest private house in the town.

Market Cross: Nearly 500 years old, the market cross was built, it is recorded, for poor market folks to stand dry when rain cometh!

High Street: The street once contained many public houses, almost all of which have now changed their use. The exception is the King's Arms Hotel, reached via an archway into a courtyard. On the opposite side, The George Veterinary Hospital was once an eighteenth-century coaching inn.

Almshouses: A hospital was first founded on this site in the late thirteenth century by the Order of St John of Jerusalem. At the Dissolution of the Monasteries, the Order was banished and the buildings were later bought by the Capital Burgesses, who donated £10 a year for the provision of almshouses on the site. The old archway is all that remains from the original hospital building. The inscription above it records the Burgesses' gift of £10.

Cross Hayes: The word Hayes means 'common' and this area was the market place for the town from Saxon times until quite recently. At Queen Victoria's Jubilee the area was turned into an outdoor dining room for the whole town.

Near the River Avon

START Lower Woodford (north end), SP4 6NH, GR SU126353

DISTANCE 3 miles (5km)

SUMMARY Easy

MAPS OS Landranger 184 Salisbury & The Plain; OS Explorer 130 Salisbury & Stonehenge

WHERE TO EAT AND DRINK
The Wheatsheaf Inn, Lower Woodford, T01722-782203

An easy walk through rich water meadows with fine views over Salisbury Plain.

START At the northern end of the village turn up the side road opposite a long thatched wall. Just before you reach the farm buildings, turn left along a footpath and follow it between fields and past a wood on the left. Continue across the next field to the road.

1 Follow the road to the junction with Wilton Rd, where you turn left down a private, gated road through the estate of Little Durnford Manor. You will eventually emerge through a door in a wall. Cross the road and continue up the lane by a wood.

2 Turn left at the crossroads by Keeper's Cottage and continue along the bridleway to a copse. Go ahead through the trees and turn left just before a gate. Follow the footpath down the hill, keeping the fence on your right. The path ends beside a farmyard and emerges onto the road.

3 Turn left and then immediately right down a lane, marked as a bridleway, by the post box. This crosses three bridges on the way back to Lower Woodford and the starting point.

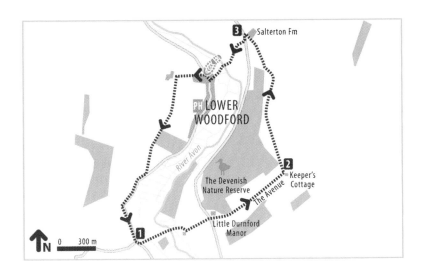

Oare & Martinsell Hill

START Oare, SN8 4JA, GR SU158631

DISTANCE 3 miles (5km)

SUMMARY Short but strenuous

MAPS OS Landranger 173 Swindon & Devizes; OS Explorer 157 Marlborough & Savernake Forest

WHERE TO EAT AND DRINK The White Hart, Oare, T01672-562273

A steep climb (and equally steep descent) to reach attractive downland with spectacular views.

START Cross the main road in Oare and go southeast along Pound La for a short distance. Rising to the left is a hill that appears to be a more distinct peak than is usual in downland. This summit is your first objective.

[1] Beyond the village houses, and opposite another track coming in from a field on the right, look out for a stile on the left with waymarks for the Mid Wilts Way and White Horse Trail. Cross the field to another stile. The track now heads quite purposefully to the top. Climb steeply to the trig point, by which time it will be obvious that the peak is merely the end of a prominent shoulder of the flat-topped upland of Martinsell Hill. After admiring the views of the Pewsey Vale and recovering your breath, continue on more level ground, crossing a barrow known as Giant's Grave. The large house in the depression to the left is the late Georgian Rainscombe House. On reaching a gate and stile, bear slightly left, following a 'Martinsell' signpost. Bear left again around the clump of trees at the top of the hill.

[2] Turn left into a broad grassy track, with a fence on your left. This track bends sharply to the left at the end of the field, where the outer bank of Martinsell hill fort is visible under the trees ahead. Follow the track along Oare Hill, then go straight across the main road and follow the bridleway sign along another track for about ½ mile. The track goes left by the entrance to Huish Down Farm.

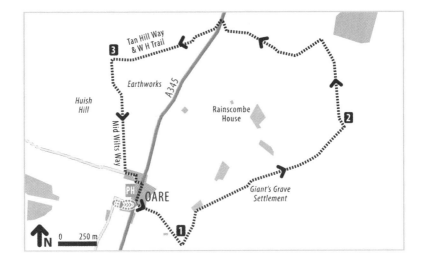

⬛3️⃣ As it bends right, go straight on along a footpath between a fence and a hedge. Just beyond the pond on the right, go through a wooden gate and continue straight down Huish Hill, aiming directly for Oare village. Halfway down, on the rim of an earthwork, a seat is placed in a strategic position. Below the seat, the path continues down the grassy hillside in an uncomfortably steep descent. When the ground levels, the path leads along the side of a field to the road by the school. Turn left, then right at the main road, passing the White Hart Inn, to return to the start.

Points of interest

Oare House is a small mansion of 1740, with wings added in the 1920s by Clough Williams-Ellis (of Portmeirion fame). The church is red-brick Victorian.

Drew's Pond & Potterne Woods

START Lay-by on A360
between Devizes and Potterne,
SN10 5LN, GR ST998591

DISTANCE 3¼ miles (5km)

SUMMARY Easy, mainly
on tracks and by-ways

MAPS OS Landranger 173
Swindon & Devizes; OS Explorer
130 Salisbury & Stonehenge,
143 Warminster & Trowbridge, 156
Chippenham & Bradford-on-Avon,
157 Marlborough & Savernake Forest

WHERE TO EAT AND DRINK
The George and Dragon,
Potterne, To1380-722139
(closed Mon–Tue lunchtimes)

A short, pleasant ramble on elevated ground and through ancient woodland,
with an optional detour into an award-winning nature reserve.

START Take the broad track from the Devizes end of the lay-by, signposted
'Drew's Pond Lane 1'. On reaching Montecello Farmhouse at the top of the
track, take the footpath on the right between two sets of farm gates and
follow the obvious path along the edge of a field.

1 Shortly after entering woodland you reach a junction. Our route is
to the right, but a short detour to the left drops down to Drew's Pond, a
charming small lake that gives its name to the surrounding nature reserve,
which can be explored along well-marked paths through the woods.
Returning to the route, the path climbs steadily along the edge of a field.
On emerging from a wooded section, there is a gap in the fence on the
left. Take this and carry on for about ½ mile on elevated ground, with
views over Devizes to Roundway Hill beyond.

2 On reaching a broad cart-track, turn right and at a junction turn
right again to reach Potterne Woods. Turn right yet again and follow the
byway along the edge of the woodland, with occasional long views to
Salisbury Plain.

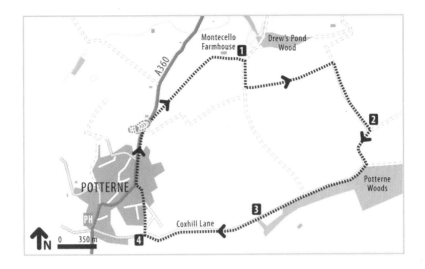

3 At a meeting of several broad trackways bear gently right downhill. This is Coxhill La, which descends through a surprisingly deep and leafy cutting towards Potterne.

4 At the first road junction, swing right then left along a path protected by bollards (not up the steps), continuing along a quiet road past the youth club to reach the A360 near the general store. Turn right to return to the lay-by, ⅓ mile up the main road. (This route bypasses the village centre; if you wish to make a detour to Porch House, the church and the pub, continue to the end of Coxhill La at the road junction 4.)

Points of interest

Drew's Pond Wood is a local nature reserve with 7.5 acres of ancient woodland, interpretation boards and a picnic area.
The large village of Potterne has a good Early English church. Porch House is a well-preserved, half-timbered, fifteenth-century building on the main street. Church House, by the church gates, dates from 1614.

Wardour Castle & Woods

START Old Wardour Castle car park, near Tisbury, SP3 6RR, GR ST941271

DISTANCE 3½ miles (5.5km)

SUMMARY Easy

MAPS OS Landranger 184 Salisbury & The Plain; OS Explorer 118 Shaftesbury & Cranborne Chase

WHERE TO EAT AND DRINK
The Forester, Donhead St Andrew, T01747-828038 (award-winning food, menu changes daily)

Well-defined field paths and woodland tracks in the Nadder Valley, starting from a romantic ruin.

START Cross the road from the car park and take the track to Ark Farm, with the lake on your left. Walk between the farm buildings and follow the track downhill until it turns left.

[1] Here, cross the stile beside a farm gate to the right and follow the field edge until you reach a fence corner, then go straight on along a well-defined track to a stile that takes you into the grounds of New Wardour Castle (now converted into apartments). Follow the curving drive past the main building and the hexagonal lodge beyond, then turn left on a footpath up two steps in the low wall. This leads to the left of a statue and a large neo-Georgian building, then through a sparse wood to a stile. Cross the stile into a field and walk diagonally left across it towards the red-tiled roof of Westfield Farm, which soon comes into view. In the boundary fence to the right of the farmhouse there is a stile and another immediately opposite. Cross these and cross the field to a farm gate in a cross-fence by a ditch.

[2] Go over another stile, crossing a stream at the edge of a wood. With the wood and fence on your left continue to Park Gate Farm. Go through the gate and between hedges to the farmyard. Cross the yard and a farm road, then go through the gate on the bank to the left. Turn left and walk up the field to the top left-hand corner to pass through a gate into a woodland clearing. Walk through the clearing to the top right-hand corner and turn right onto a well-defined path that leads through the wood and across a field to a stony track.

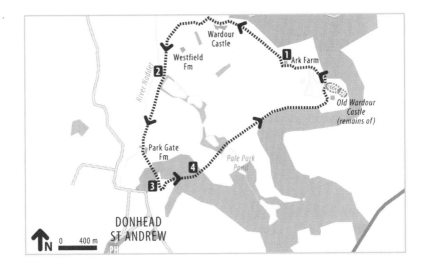

[3] Turn right here to walk down to the village of Donhead St Andrew if you want to visit the Forester pub; otherwise turn left past Pile Oak Lodge to reach the entrance to Wardour Wood. Go along the track to where it bears right.

[4] Turn left on a path leading down through a gate and out of the wood across a field to another gate. Go straight on, following the edge of Pale Park pond. Continue through an opening, keeping close to the fence, left, then go on with the wood on your right. Join a well-defined track and follow it back to Old Wardour Castle.

Points of interest

Old Wardour Castle, built in the fourteenth century by Lord Lovell, subsequently became the home, for some 400 years, of the Arundell family, of whom Lady Blanche was the most famous. With a total compliment of around twenty-nine souls, she held out against a besieging force of 1,300 Parliamentarian troops for nearly ten days, before being forced to surrender. The castle is now administered by English Heritage and is open for most of the year.

Easton Grey to Pinkney

START Easton Grey, south of the B4040 Sherston–Malmesbury road, SN16 0PJ, GR ST880873

DISTANCE 3½ miles (6km)

SUMMARY Easy

MAPS OS Landranger 173 Swindon & Devizes; OS Explorer 168 Stroud, Tetbury & Malmesbury

WHERE TO EAT AND DRINK There are no pubs on the route, but The Rattlebone Inn, T01666-840871, is just up the B4040 in Sherston (food served daily; dogs welcome in public bar)

A short, pleasant walk through Wiltshire farmland.

START The houses of the tiny hamlet of Easton Grey are exceptionally pretty and in typical Cotswold style. Walk downhill to the bridge to cross the river. A short way beyond the bridge, pass through the gate on the right and go straight up the path between the trees and into the large field beyond. At the top of the incline, head across the field with a fence to your right towards the small copse above the river, and look to your right for a superb view of Easton Grey House. Just to the left of the copse go over a stile, a footbridge and a second stile and continue in the same direction across the next field, walking to the left of the group of trees to a farm gate in the opposite corner.

① Go downhill with the hedge on your left and cross a stile. Continue across the next two fields in the same direction, and go over the stile in the hedge ahead. Turn left to follow the enclosed footpath around the paddock to a gate that opens onto a farm track.

② Turn left through the gate on the signed footpath leading up the hill away from Park Farm. Proceed for about ½ mile, keeping the stone wall of Pinkney Park on your right and passing a large metal gate in the estate wall. Go through a farm gate and continue until you pass a double set of wooden rails, then bear left towards the metal gate in the hedge in front of you and turn left at the road.

③ Keep to the road for about a mile, passing New Barn Farm on your left and going straight over the crossroads.

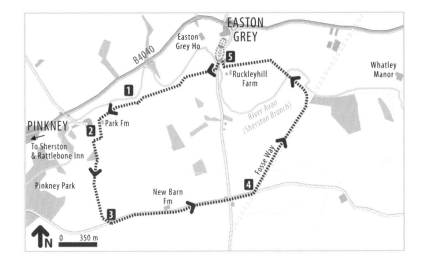

④ About 200yds further on, a track crosses the road. This is, in fact, the ancient Fosse Way. Turn left along it and continue until it starts to descend to the river, then go left through a farm gate into a field and follow the grassy track veering diagonally left. This beautiful stretch of countryside, close to the River Avon, is the site of an ancient Roman settlement, though not a trace of it can be seen. As you reach the next gate, among trees, look back and right for a fine view of Whatley Manor, now a hotel. Pass through the gate and follow the track ahead, keeping to the hedge on your right. After the next gate, continue straight ahead to another gate, passing between ruined buildings, then cross the bridge near the weir. From the bridge, take the small path leading uphill and follow it as it leads along the edge of the next field. At the end of the field go through a gate on the left and cross the field to a stile.

⑤ Continue across the next field towards farm buildings. Go through the gate in the fence to return to the road in Easton Grey.

Points of interest

The Roman Fosse Way ran from Lincoln to Exeter and is so named because it was bordered on both sides by a 'fosse' or ditch.

Highworth to Sevenhampton

START Highworth Market Sq, SN6 7AA, GR SU202925 (parking available in Brewery St or Cherry Orchard)

DISTANCE 3½ miles (5.5km)

SUMMARY Easy

MAPS OS Landranger 174 Newbury & Wantage; OS Explorer 170 Abingdon, Wantage & Vale of White Horse

WHERE TO EAT AND DRINK Numerous places to suit all budgets in Highworth

START Starting in the Market Sq with the church to your right, cross the High St and go through the large archway and continue along Gilberts La past the supermarket to Brewery St beyond. Cross the road and walk down the length of Kings Av opposite, then on into the school playing field, and walk alongside the fence separating the school buildings to the right. Cross the stile into the field and turn right, then follow left round the clump of trees to a stile into another field.

1 The footpath initially starts with the hedge on your right and then continues in a straight line across the field to the farm track (it may be easier to follow the line of the hedge all the way to the track). Turn right and cross the road and then walk down the drive to the golf club.

2 Just past the clubhouse turn left through a gap in the hedge and, following marked posts, cross the fairway to the gap in the middle of the trees and continue in a straight line across another fairway, again keeping the next hedge to your left.

3 Enter a field through a metal kissing gate and after a few yards go through a metal gate in the hedge and turn right.

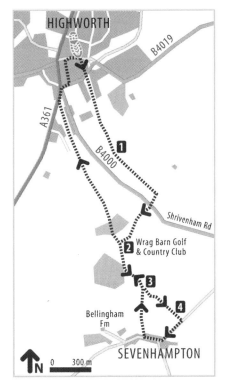

④ After approximately 150yds, go through the gap on the right between the hedge and fence into the garden of a house. Walk through to the drive and out onto the road, turning right down the hill. Follow the pavement round to the right and, just before the phone box, turn right at a fingerpost along a path between houses and into the field beyond. Walk up the field, heading for the metal gate in the top left-hand corner ③ and retrace your steps back through the golf course to the gap in the hedge near the clubhouse ②. Now continue in the same direction across two fairways to a gap in the trees to a fenced path between fields. On reaching the houses, the path becomes a metalled surface. Follow this to the main road and turn right to the roundabout. Cross into Brewery St and take the second turning left into Blandford Alley, which eventually emerges into the High St. Turn right to get back to Market Sq.

Points of interest

The grave of James Bond author Ian Fleming is in Sevenhampton churchyard.

The Winterbournes

START South of Winterbourne
Earls church, SP4 6EZ, GR
SU175344 (park in lay-by)

DISTANCE 3½ miles (6km)

SUMMARY Easy

MAPS OS Landranger 184
Salisbury & The Plain; OS Explorer
130 Salisbury & Stonehenge

WHERE TO EAT AND DRINK
The Black House, Black Horse La,
Hurdcott, T01980-619089; The
Winterbourne Arms, Winterbourne
Dauntsey, T01980-611306

A gentle stroll in the valley of the River Bourne.

START Walk south along the road for about ½ mile and, where the pavement ends, turn right through a small gate, following a signpost to Hurdcott, across a paddock and between fields on a grassy track. At the end of this track turn right along the road and then left into a bridleway as the road bends right. Pass a small pumping station, cross the River Bourne and, by the entrance to the sewage treatment works, take a narrow path straight ahead. Almost immediately turn right through a gate and continue along the edge of a field. On reaching a metalled track, carry on, taking a wide track ahead in 50yds when the main track bends right.

1 At the next metalled road, where there is a ford to the right, turn left for 60yds and go through a gap in the hedge on the right. Carry straight on through another gate. Cross another metalled road, and then follow a track along the hedgerow on the right of the field. As the field boundary bends left, go through a gate on the right. Proceed diagonally across a small field to a stile leading to the main road.

2 Turn right along the road and right again at the roundabout into Winterbourne Gunner. Note the grassy track on the left, which leads to the very attractive small church. Turn left at the road junction and left again through a kissing gate to follow a field path towards Gomeldon, the site of a medieval village.

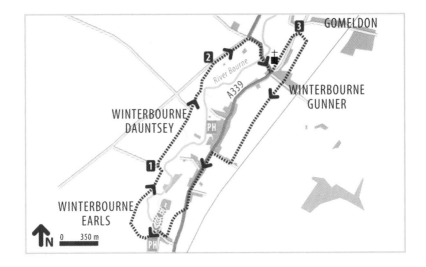

③ Rejoin the road by another gate and, in 100yds, turn right down a few steps to follow a path bending gradually to the right. Carry on through gaps in the hedges and then follow a generally straight line for almost 1 mile, passing through a residential area on the way. At the second metalled road turn right to return to the main road at Winterbourne Earls church. The starting point is a short distance to the left.

Points of interest

Winterbourne Gunner has a well-situated, largely thirteenth-century church, with a Norman tower.

The nineteenth-century church in Winterbourne Earls was built by Wyatt to replace demolished churches at Winterbourne Earls and Winterbourne Dauntsey, re-using materials from both medieval buildings.

Great Bedwyn & the Brails

START Church St, Great Bedwyn,
SN8 3PG, GR SU277643

DISTANCE 3½ miles (6km)

SUMMARY Easy

MAPS OS Landranger 174 Newbury
& Wantage; OS Explorer 157
Marlborough & Savernake Forest

WHERE TO EAT AND DRINK The Cross
Keys, Great Bedwyn, T01672-870678
(classic, inexpensive pub food)

An easy walk along a canal towpath and through woods.

START Just beyond the church in Great Bedwyn is a signpost to Bedwyn
Brail. Take this path, going through a wooden gate into an extension of
the churchyard. Go through a narrow V-stile into a field. Walk straight
across and you will come to two kissing gates, which take you over the
railway (this is very much in use, so watch out for trains) and then to
the Kennet and Avon Canal and the River Dun. Cross the bridge and
turn right by the lock, then follow the towpath for about ¾ mile, going
underneath a bridge.

① When you come to a second bridge (New Bridge) and another lock,
turn left and walk along the right side of the field towards the wood ahead
(Wilton Brail). At the edge of the wood there are footpaths signed both to
the left and straight ahead. Go through a V-stile into the wood and walk
straight ahead for a few yards until you come to a metalled track. Bear left
up the track. When you come to a road, turn right and walk along it for a
few yards.

② At the bend, turn left through a hedge gap onto a grass path running
between fences. Here you can see Wilton Windmill about ¼ mile away
to your right. When the path forks, bear left along the bridleway into the
wood, passing a pond on your right. Follow the path through the clearing
to a junction of footpaths and follow the sign to Great Bedwyn until
you come to a metalled track. Here, turn left past the Bedwyn Brail sign
(which states that dogs must be kept on leads). Follow the track through
Bedwyn Brail for about 1 mile (you may see deer).

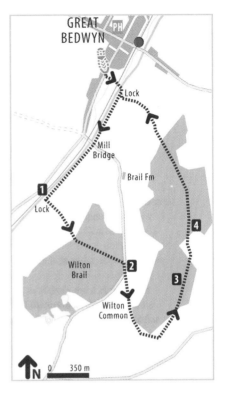

③ At one point you will pass the top of a broad grass drive from which you can see Tottenham House and possibly a monument on the skyline beyond, some 4 miles away at the edge of Savernake Forest. Go straight on, crossing a large clearing and, when the track forks bear left, keeping to the metalled track (signed to Great Bedwyn). Shortly, the track peters out into a grassy path in another clearing. Go straight on.

④ Then, when the path diverges before reaching more trees, take the left fork. Follow this narrow path down through the wood until you come to a field. Make for the far left corner of the field ahead and continue through a gap into another field. You can now see the village of Great Bedwyn ahead. Continue along the left side of the field down a small hill until you come to the canal and the lock where you started the walk. Retrace your steps over the bridge and the railway, through the churchyard and back to Church St.

Points of interest

The church of St Mary the Virgin in Great Bedwyn is built entirely of flint. The nave and chancel are the oldest parts and date from the late twelfth century. It contains a monument to Sir John Seymour, father of Henry VIII's third wife Jane Seymour, whose family seat was nearby Wolfhall.

Ramsbury & Littlecote

START The Bell, Ramsbury,
SN8 2PE, GR SU275715

DISTANCE 4 miles (6.5km)

SUMMARY Easy

MAPS OS Landranger 174 Newbury
& Wantage; OS Explorer 157
Marlborough & Savernake Forest,
158 Newbury & Hungerford

WHERE TO EAT AND DRINK
The Bell, Ramsbury, T01672-
520230 (award-winning pub with
restaurant and rooms; also has
a mud room and welly washer;
dogs welcome); Café Bella, behind
The Bell (cosy, serves homemade
breakfasts, soups, cakes, etc.)

An easy-to-follow circuit in parkland and woods, all on very good tracks.

START Walk down Scholard's La (following the sign to Hungerford), and turn right on the Froxfield road to cross the River Kennet, which is most attractive at this point. In a short distance, just before a house on the left, leave the road by a metalled track signposted 'Littlecote House'.

1 Keep left at a junction just beyond the house, following the line of the river. On reaching West Lodge, carry on, with the river now closer.

2 The grounds of Littlecote House are soon reached, in which the extensive remains of a Roman villa lie between the track and the river. Just beyond the Roman remains, at a junction of tracks, turn right past a timber and thatch house, heading for a belt of woodland.

3 When you reach the trees, turn right opposite a 'Private' sign, and proceed slightly uphill. At two ensuing junctions, bear right on each occasion. The countryside is now particularly attractive.

4 At the top of the hill, leave the metalled track as it bends to the right and go straight on along the footpath at the edge of the wood. Follow this delightful track downwards through the trees, with Ramsbury coming into view across the valley. Rejoin the original track at the house 1 and turn right at the road to return to Ramsbury.

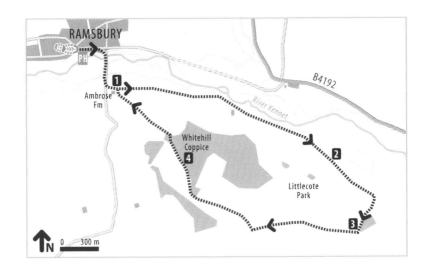

Points of interest

Littlecote House is Elizabethan, now a hotel. The remains of the Roman villa in its park are open to the public and include the fourth-century 'Orpheus' mosaic, restored in 1979–80 from detailed drawings made when it was first uncovered in 1727.

Ramsbury is a large village with many thatched cottages and other good buildings. The impressive church has Saxon remains.

Around Wilton

START The Swan, Wilton,
SN8 3SS, GR SU267715

DISTANCE 4 miles (6.5km)

SUMMARY Easy

MAPS OS Landranger 174 Newbury
& Wantage; OS Explorer 157
Marlborough & Savernake Forest

WHERE TO EAT AND DRINK
The Swan, Wilton, T01672-870274;
Engineman's Rest Café,
Crofton Pumping Station

A short, pleasant walk through woodland and along a canal towpath.

START From The Swan follow the main street in the direction of Great
Bedwyn (see Walk 9), and, after leaving the village, take the second
turning on the right, signposted to Shalbourne and Wilton Windmill. The
track leading to the windmill is about ¼ mile along this road on the right.

[1]   Continue past the windmill to the next turning on the right,
signposted to Marten. Turn left here down a grassy track between the
trees. Turn right at the first fork (by a small pond) and bear right again
(signed to Great Bedwyn) when you reach a clearing on the left.

[2]   Continue to a wide metalled track, and turn left along it for ¼
mile through Bedwyn Brail. As a clearing opens out in the trees to the
right, allowing views of the countryside beyond, take the broad, grassy
track leading downhill to the left, signed to Wilton Brail. From here, the
imposing Tottenham House is just visible in the distance. At the edge of
the wood, go through a hedge gap and cross the field to the gate opposite.
Cross the road beyond and continue straight on along the track through
Wilton Brail, heading in the same direction until the estate road curves
left near the edge of the wood.

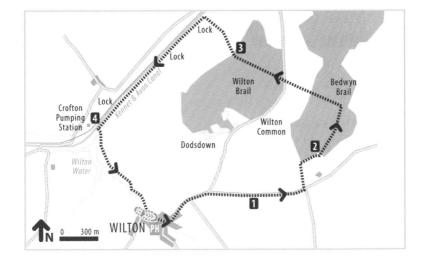

3　Leave the road here and cross a stile by a gate to the right at the bottom of the slope. Cross the field beyond, keeping the fence on your left, to the gate beside the canal towpath. Turn left along the towpath and follow the course of the canal until you cross a track near a level crossing. Just beyond here, on the other side of the canal, is the Crofton Pumping Station, a working museum that is well worth a visit. It can be reached by crossing the canal at the next lock.

4　Just before the lock by the pumping station, take the path to the left signed to Wilton Windmill. The path follows the course of Wilton Water and takes you back to the road running through Wilton. Turn left to return to the Swan Inn.

Points of interest

 Wilton Windmill, restored and producing flour, can be viewed from outside at all times and is open 2–5pm on Sun and Bank Holiday Mon from Easter to end Sept (dogs welcome).

At the fascinating working museum of Crofton Pumping Station it is possible to see the oldest beam engine still capable of being operated. It was used to pump water into the Kennet and Avon Canal by means of steam power, and the huge pistons and beams are an impressive sight. The museum is open daily Easter–Oct, with a number of steaming weekends (T01672-870300, croftonbeamengines.org).

Coate Water

START Car park at Coate Water
Country Park, SN3 6AA, GR SU177826

DISTANCE 4 miles (6.5km);
longer route 6 miles (9.5km),
shorter route 2 miles (3.25km)

MAPS OS Landranger 173
Swindon & Devizes; OS Explorer
169 Cirencester & Swindon

SUMMARY Easy

WHERE TO EAT AND DRINK The Sun
Inn, T01793-523292 (just off the Coate
Water roundabout); The Holiday Inn
Hotel, T01793-524601 (opposite the
Sun); The Spotted Cow, T01793-485832
(with a large children's play garden)

An easy walk mostly over well-made paths and level ground.

START From the car park go up to the lake and turn left and follow the
path to cross the dam at the far end of the lake.

1️⃣ Bear left, following signs for Hodson/Chisledon. At the end of the
track, the path goes right and then left to become a metalled surface to the
spiral footbridge over the M4. Having crossed the bridge, turn left and go
through a metal kissing gate into a field. Cross the field diagonally to the
corner, then go through another kissing gate and follow the path right,
through a wood and up the hill. Continue along the path through the field
with the hedge on your right. At the end of the field, the path slopes down.

2️⃣ A few paces down the slope turn right by a small oak tree, then left
through a metal gate. This next section can be very muddy after rain; see
'Drier alternative route' below. Continue down the slope, over a stile and
into a field. Keep in the same direction down the field and cross the bridge
over the ditch and immediately turn right along the valley bottom.

3️⃣ Go through a gate with a wood on your right. Follow the line of trees
as it bears right, then go through a gate and bridge on the right. Bear left
and climb the bank, then continue diagonally across the field, through a
line of trees and a gate into a wood. Bear left up to the top of the slope to
meet a cross track.

4️⃣ Turn left and follow the path, then as it starts to descend and bear
left, go through a gap in the hedge on the right. Turn left along the field
edge and follow the wood on the left to reach a road, but stay in the field
to a stile just before a barn and phone mast. Go over and right along the

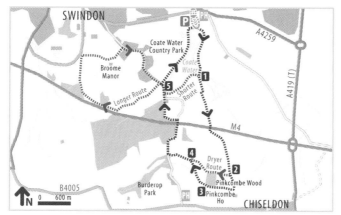

road. Immediately after the road crosses the motorway, turn left into a thicket and follow the path down and right, then through a gate into a field. Walk to the opposite side of the field, then turn right away from the motorway, keeping the fence and wood on the left, to a gate at the end of the field. Go out through the gate and diagonally across the sharp corner of the road. Turn left along a path to the end of the hedge that separates the path from the road.

⑤ Turn right between the trees back into Coate Water Country Park, then continue through an avenue of trees to the lake. Follow the lake to the diving board and snack bar then down to the car park at the start.

Shorter route: Go right at waypoint ① and circumnavigate the lake as far as the road. Turn right and continue from waypoint ⑤.

Longer route: Go left at ⑤ and head along the wooded track signposted 'Old Town Railway Path and Lydiard Country Park', with the golf course on your right. Follow this until it runs alongside the M4 and continue to where a footbridge crosses the motorway on the left. A few steps beyond, turn right and follow the track to the road. Turn right along the golf club drive and head round the back to the far side of the clubhouse. At the playing area, turn left following the 'Walkers this way' sign. Follow this to the road, then turn right and head back to waypoint ⑤.

Drier alternative route: After going through the gate at ②, turn right up a gradual slope, go along the edge of a bank through trees, then pass through another gate into a field. Continue in the same direction along the field edge. Ignore the path from the left, and a bit further on bear left through a gate to leave the field and continue through the trees at the top of the bank to the point where another path joins on the left ④.

Cherhill Down

START Knoll Down near
Beckhampton (park in lay-by
on A4), SN8 1QR, GR SU077692

DISTANCE 4 miles (6.5km)
or 6 miles (10km)

SUMMARY Moderate with
some hilly walking

MAPS OS Landranger 173 Swindon
& Devizes; OS Explorer 157
Marlborough & Savernake Forest

WHERE TO EAT AND DRINK
The Black Horse, Cherhill,
T01249-813365; The Waggon and
Horses, Beckhampton, T01672-529418
(just past the roundabout on
the A4 Marlborough road)

A breezy downland walk on grassy trackways with spacious views and ancient earthworks.

START Walk to the end of the lay-by and pass through the trees towards a grassy track that leads right towards a beech wood on higher ground. Go through the wood and keep straight on, with fine views first to the south and later to the north and west. (There are two tracks here: a broad one to the right running between fences, and a lower one to the left. It does not matter which is followed and they eventually join.) Just past a tumulus, the track begins to descend and another chalky track comes up from the main road below.

1 Turn left onto this and gradually climb the downs towards another beech wood on the right skyline. Soon a barn and reservoir is reached, with a gate and stile on the right. Cross this stile and follow the track as it climbs uphill. A National Trust sign to the left of the track announces 'Cherhill Down and Oldbury Castle'. Through the gate, the fence on the right ends after about 50yds and if you wish you can strike off right of the track to the mighty ditch and ramparts of Oldbury Castle.

2 Walk to the left along the grassy track and through the central part of the hill fort to the Lansdowne Monument.

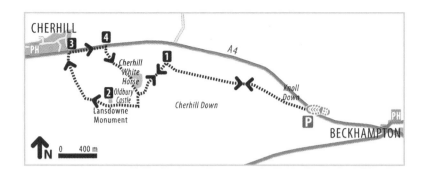

③ To extend the walk, take the track that runs behind the monument to descend to the A4, with views of the White Horse to your right. Turn left to reach the Black Horse pub in Cherhill. To return, walk back along the main road to Poachers Croft.

④ Take the track uphill signposted to Oldbury Castle. Follow the grassy path up the spine of the hill to the left of the track, up around the White Horse and past the copse on your left, to return to the hill fort. You are recommended to return to the car park by the same route, as the views in this direction are perhaps even more spectacular than on the outward walk.

Points of interest

Oldbury Castle is an Iron Age hill fort of majestic size.
The stone obelisk called the Lansdowne Monument commemorates Sir William Petty, a seventeenth-century physician and surveyor, and was erected by the 3rd Marquis of Lansdowne, a descendant of Petty.
The chalk Cherhill White Horse was first cut in 1780.

Mildenhall & the River Kennet

START Mildenhall village hall,
SN8 2LR, GR SU213698

DISTANCE 4 miles (6.5km)

SUMMARY Easy

MAPS OS Landranger 174 Newbury
& Wantage; OS Explorer 157
Marlborough & Savernake Forest

WHERE TO EAT AND DRINK
The Horseshoe Inn, Mildenhall,
T01672-514725

A short walk with good views over the Kennet valley and a stretch along the riverside.

START Follow the road through Mildenhall towards Ramsbury until a right turn leads to a bridge over the River Kennet. Follow the lane uphill to a T-junction. Turn left and in a very short distance slant right up the drive across the front of a house.

① Beyond the double gates, carry on uphill on a good path, known as Cock-a-troop La. Near the top of the hill, turn left on a crossing path and follow it along the top of a field, with open views over the Kennet valley.

② In about 600yds, Hill Barn is reached among trees. Turn right and follow the farm track past the now derelict buildings. Immediately beyond the gap in the hedge, turn left and follow the hedgerow along the side of a large field to a road. Cross and continue in the same direction, again with the hedge on your left. On reaching Oxleaze Copse, carry on beside it to the far end of the wood, then go straight on through the hedgerow and across two stiles. Turn left into the lane beyond the stiles and go downhill.

③ Fork right at the bottom corner of the wood, then pass Coombe Farm. On reaching a metalled road (Kings Dr), turn left along it. As the road turns sharply left, carry straight on over a stile and cross a small field to a stile on the far side near cottages.

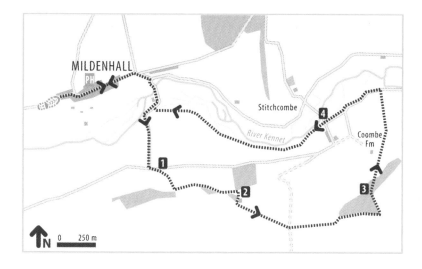

④ Cross the Stitchcombe road and follow a path, signposted to Werg, along the side of the river. As the river bends to the right, cross a stile ahead and continue by a lightly used path near the hedge. On the left is the Blackfield, site of the Roman town of Cunetio. The path ends at a stile leading to the road. Turn right to cross the river and return to the starting point.

18 Westwood & Farleigh Hungerford

START Westwood Manor National Trust car park, BA15 2AF, GR ST812589

DISTANCE 4 miles (6.5km)

SUMMARY Easy walk in fields and lanes

MAPS OS Landranger 173 Swindon & Devizes; OS Explorer 156 Chippenham & Bradford-on-Avon

WHERE TO EAT AND DRINK The New Inn, Lower Westwood, T01225-863123; The Hungerford Arms, Farleigh Hungerford, T01225-781221; Stowford Manor Farm serves cream teas daily 3–6pm, Easter to end Oct

A lovely and exhilarating walk across open countryside, visiting an old castle.

START Leave the car park and turn left along the road for 20yds. Now turn left over a barred stile and head across the field beyond in the direction of the fingerpost pointing to Stowford. At the far side, go to the left of a small pond, then through a gap and maintain direction across the next field. Cross a stile and continue. There are good views from here: if it is clear you may be able to see the Westbury White Horse in the distance. At the far side of the field, go over a barred stile to the left of a gate, and bear slightly right down the next field, aiming towards the left-hand corner of a hedge coming in from the right. Continue down the field to reach a gap in the low hedge ahead. Go through and bear left along a farm track. The track crosses a small stream and then turns right. Continue along the track, with the stream on your right, to reach the A366.

[1] Cross the road with care, and turn right for 100yds to reach the entrance to Stowford Manor Farm. Here, turn left into the drive for 10yds, then turn right across a field. Although not shown on the map, there is a path over this open access land that runs between the A366, on the right, and the River Frome, which soon appears on the left. On this section of the walk you cross into Somerset. Soon you will be able to see the tower of Farleigh Castle ahead. Go through a kissing gate to reach the Farleigh & District Swimming Club by a weir on the Frome, then continue across the next field to reach a stile leading back to the road near a junction.

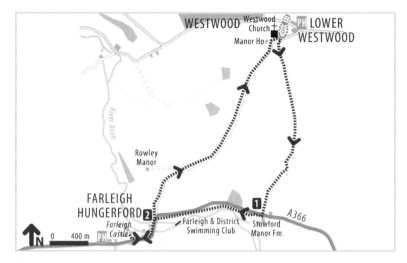

② To visit the castle, turn left, go over two road bridges, and follow the road as it bends right uphill. The entrance to the castle is at the top of the hill on the right. From the castle, turn left and retrace your steps to the road junction. Now, go straight ahead up a minor road, past Rowley Cottage. The road ascends fairly steeply and, at the top, you may catch glimpses of Rowley Manor through the hedgerow to your left. Continue to reach a lodge on the left. About 500yds further on, to the right, is the site of a medieval village, though you will need a good imagination as there is very little to be seen. Continue to reach Westwood church and Manor, where the walk ends, or go on a little further to reach the New Inn at the next junction.

Points of interest

The remains of Farleigh castle sit peacefully on a hill. The first castle dates from the fourteenth century. It has sixteenth-century stained-glass windows of exceptional quality, a crypt with eight lead coffins, and the tomb of Sir Thomas Hungerford, who built the castle. Managed by English Heritage, it is open daily 10am–6pm Apr–Sept and 10am–5pm Oct, weekends only 10am–4pm Nov–Mar.

Westwood Manor House (National Trust, open Apr–Sept, Tue, Wed and Sun, 2–5pm) is a lovely old house rich in curiosities. It dates from the fifteenth century and has fine Jacobean windows and topiary. The Manor, and the church of St Mary the Virgin which stands beside it, complement each other in their quiet idyllic appearance.

19 Bremhill & Maud Heath's Highway

START St Martin's church,
Bremhill, SN11 9LB, GR ST978731

DISTANCE 4 miles (6.5km)

SUMMARY Easy walk on
well-marked paths

MAPS OS Landranger 173 Swindon
& Devizes; OS Explorer 156
Chippenham & Bradford-on-Avon

WHERE TO EAT AND DRINK The
Dumb Post, Bremhill, T01249-813192
(Sat–Sun open all day, closed Mon)

A delightful walk through rolling hills along broad, grassy paths, with splendid views throughout.

START Go down the main street to the bottom of the hill. As the road begins to go uphill, go past the farm entrance and through the kissing gate on the left. Cross the field to a stile and plank bridge on the opposite side. Bear right towards the brow of the hill and through a plantation. Go through the gate near the telegraph pole ahead of you, and turn left at the road. Take the first turning on the right, signposted 'Charlcutt', looking to the right for a good view of the downs beyond Calne. Pass some houses on the left.

1   About 50yds before you reach some barns, turn sharp left through a gate and along a bridleway into a field. Keeping the hedge on your right, cross the field to the next gate. Continue in the same direction through several more fields, always following the line of the fences and hedges, until you reach the monument to Maud Heath. The views from the monument and all along this stretch of the walk are superb. From the monument, continue in the same direction as before towards the farm surrounded by pine trees. Cross the road and pass through the gateway opposite, where another inscription to Maud Heath is mounted on the stone pillar on the right. Make for the clump of trees ahead and, keeping to the left side of the wood, pass through several more fields until you reach another wood directly in front of you. Bear left just in front of the trees to the first gate on the right, from which there are fine views across the valley to Derry Hill.

2   Turn left at the road and pass Bencroft Farm. Opposite the adjacent Old Coach House, go through a wooden gate and follow the marked footpath to the left over a stile, passing a pond on your right. Cross another stile to the right to enter the wood. Turn right downhill at the crossing path, then left just before the wooden gate to continue along the path

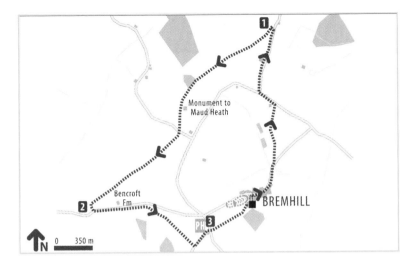

that follows the edge of the wood, with open views to the right, until you emerge on the road via the drive of Thimble Hall. Turn left and walk up the hill, passing the Dumb Post Inn on your right. This pub commands good views from its lounge bar and has seats outside in its pleasant garden.

③   At the T-junction, cross the road and take the footpath that begins as the garage drive of the house just opposite the pub sign. Go through the squeeze stile to the left of the garage and follow the left-hand hedge to another stile. The path now leads through the grounds of a large, old house. Keep to the left of the tennis court and continue into the churchyard of Bremhill church, from there returning to your starting point.

Points of interest

Now part of the folklore of this area, Maud Heath lived in medieval times, and in 1474 made a bequest of land in order to build and maintain a causeway through the Avon marshes to Chippenham. Fragments of this causeway are still visible, principally at Kellaways on the Avon, where there is another monument to her. The Bremhill path was also part of her route to town.

The ancient church at Bremhill has some Saxon and Norman stonework and a twelfth-century font. Between 1804 and 1850, the vicar here was William Bowles, who was to influence the writings of Coleridge and Southey. An inscription to an old soldier on the wall of the church, together with the lines on Maud Heath's monument, were written by him.

Bradford-on-Avon to Avoncliff

START Bradford-on-Avon station car park, BA15 1DF, GR ST824606

DISTANCE 4 miles (6.5km)

SUMMARY Easy with no steep ascents

MAPS OS Landranger 173 Swindon & Devizes; OS Explorer 156 Chippenham & Bradford-on-Avon

WHERE TO EAT AND DRINK The Cross Guns, Avoncliff, T01225-862335 (food served daily, 10am–9pm); Blue Cow Café, Avoncliff (light lunches and afternoon teas served on the lawn, dogs welcome); Mr Salvat's Coffee Room, Bradford-on-Avon, T01225-867474 (authentic-feeling 17th-century coffee house with open fire and secluded garden; light lunches, home-made cakes; open Thu–Sun and bank holidays 10am–5pm)

A delightful waterside walk by the river and canal, crossing a graceful Georgian stone aqueduct.

START From the end of the car park farthest from the station take the footpath down to the river and turn left under the railway bridge. To the right can be seen the ancient Packhorse Bridge, and to the left a group of very fine fourteenth-century buildings, one of which is the Tithe Barn. Proceed along the path that starts the Country Park walk, marked by the adjacent information board. From here there are some good views of the old weavers' cottages on the hillside. Leaving Bradford behind, follow the path and the gently winding river.

1   Where the path forks, take the slight incline to the left past the sewage works and up to the Kennet and Avon canal towpath. You are still following the river, but at a higher level, with far-reaching views across to Winsley (on the right) with its sloping patchwork fields and grazing cattle.

2   The Cross Guns pub can be found at the end of the path at Avoncliff, by turning right and walking down the slope. Food and drink can be consumed outside while enjoying the spectacular weir with magnificent views of the Limpley Stoke valley, as well as the impressive Georgian aqueduct. If you prefer a cream tea, the Blue Cow Café can be found by walking under the aqueduct. To make the round trip back to Bradford-on-Avon, walk over the aqueduct (with the canal on your left) and along the lane that follows the railway line north of the river. Turn right onto

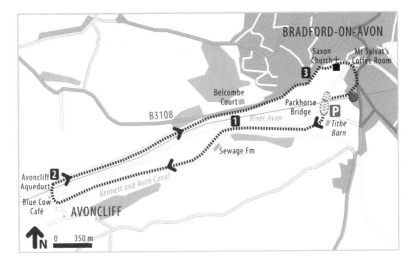

Belcombe Rd (B3108). Belcombe Court, a Georgian manor house, can be seen on the left.

③ As the road narrows and its name changes to Newtown, cross to the right and take the downhill path (by the letterbox) down to Barton Orchard – note the eighteenth-century weavers' houses. Continue down past the Chantry and at the bottom is Church St, which houses the Norman parish church and the ancient Saxon church of St Laurence. Keep to the right and follow the road to the footbridge over the river. Walk through St Margaret's car park and turn right into the main road to reach the station car park.

Points of interest

Bradford-on-Avon's Packhorse Bridge, also known as Barton Bridge, is a very good example of medieval architecture. The bridge belongs to the Barton Farm complex, as does the early fourteenth-century Tithe Barn, an impressive cathedral-like building. Despite its gargantuan proportions it has a homely feel. The early eleventh-century Saxon church is one of the most complete Saxon buildings still in existence. Holy Trinity church, opposite, is largely Norman and boasts some examples of medieval sculpture. Westbury House, across the bridge, is a fine early eighteenth-century clothier's house, once the scene of a cloth workers' riot.

Avoncliff Aqueduct was designed by John Rennie and built between 1797 and 1801 to carry the Kennet and Avon Canal over the River Avon.

A Flight of Locks Near Devizes

START The George and Dragon, Rowde, SN10 2PN, GR ST977627

DISTANCE 4 miles (6.5km)

SUMMARY Easy walk on tracks, field paths and towpath

MAPS OS Landranger 173 Swindon & Devizes; OS Explorer 156 Chippenham & Bradford-on-Avon

WHERE TO EAT AND DRINK

The George and Dragon, Rowde, T01380-723053 (with restaurant specializing in seafood); Caen Hill Café, T01380-724880 (canalside café serving soup, sandwiches, etc. near the top of the Caen Hill flight; open Mon–Fri 10.30am–4.30pm, weekends and bank holidays 10am–5pm)

A walk beside the spectacular flight of sixteen locks carrying the Kennet and Avon Canal up Caen Hill.

START From the village street, take the footpath between the George and the village hall to Rowde church. Continue through the churchyard and turn right into Rowde Court Rd, then left at the end of the houses. Follow the bridleway round to the right, on a farm track that gives way to a grassy path. Turn left over a stile and bear right down the edge of the field to a stile and footbridge. Go left and up past the lock pound.

1 Cross the canal by the bridge over the lock to reach the towpath. Turn left and follow the canal for 1½ miles to the A361 bridge.

2 Cross the bridge, then turn left and follow the private road beside the canal to the Kennet and Avon Waterways Offices.

3 Follow the track to its right to the Caen Hill top car park. Return to the canal and walk down the grassy slope beside the pounds until you reach steps down to the right leading to the car park access road. Walk down this to the road.

4 Turn right and follow the road for about ½ mile to return to Rowde.

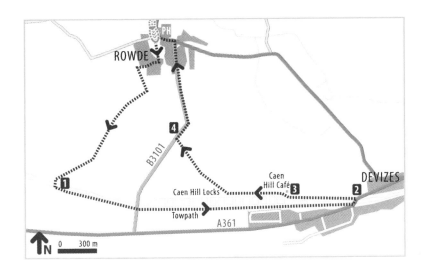

Points of interest

Caen Hill Locks, a unique flight of locks designed by John Rennie, were
built in 1810. There are twenty-nine locks in the entire Devizes flight,
sixteen of which form a giant stairway, enabling the canal to rise 237ft
in only 2 miles.

START On road leading out of
Boyton, BA12 0SS, GR ST947399

DISTANCE 4 miles (6.5km)

SUMMARY Easy

MAPS OS Landranger 184
Salisbury & The Plain; OS Explorer
143 Warminster & Trowbridge

WHERE TO EAT AND DRINK The
Trough Restaurant at the Ginger
Piggery, Boyton, T01985-850381
(Wed–Sat, 10am–5.30pm)

Fields, paths and a woodland track reaching one of the highest points on the
southern downlands.

START Follow the road away from Boyton until you reach a turning right
signposted as a no-through road. Directly opposite this turning there is a
bridleway leading left. Take this track, which climbs up through trees from
the valley some 300ft to the top of Codford Hill. Shortly after the track
levels out you will pass farm buildings on your left, and just beyond these
the track emerges onto a metalled road. Turn left and follow this road for
about a mile. Shortly after the end of the wood on the left you pass a group
of cow barns surrounded by trees and then, to your left, an ancient burial
mound just beyond a gate.

1   A little further on from this tumulus the metalled road bears right
and a rough track goes straight on. Take this descending track and about
¼ mile further on, just beyond a pair of farm gates, cross a stile on the left
and go over a similar crossing in the fence opposite. Descend the steep
slope to the boundary fence. Turn right and follow the fence to a metal
gate. Go through the gate and bear slightly left to another metal gate.

2   Go through this, cross the road and go over a stile by the gate
opposite. Cross the field, bearing slightly left towards another stile, then
go over Sherrington Mere on a bridge made of old railway sleepers. On
reaching the road, turn right and walk down to a junction by two thatched
cottages. Turn left and walk up to Rectory Cottage (Sherrington church
is a little further on around the corner). Turn left up a rough track and
follow this until you reach an opening on the left.

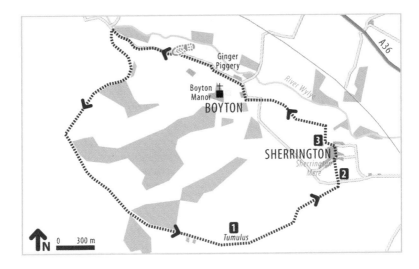

3 Go into the field ahead, turn immediately right and follow the field boundary round, under a group of trees and into the next field. Continue to follow the boundary hedge to a gate, then cross another small field to reach the road. Here, turn right and follow the road down and round the bends. Ignore the signposted road on your right opposite the main entrance to Boyton Manor and continue ahead. If you wish to visit Boyton church and Manor, turn left by a house with a post box in its wall. Otherwise continue along the road, past the Ginger Piggery on your right, back to the start.

Points of interest

The pond of Sherrington Mere was originally a watercress bed, created in the late nineteenth century by controlling springs feeding the River Wylye. Commercial production ended in 1974.

Note the Bible texts affixed to the end wall of Rectory Cottage.

Sherrington church has an unusual dedication to two Middle Eastern Saints, Damien and Cosmos. It's a fine little medieval church that's well worth a visit.

In the thirteenth-century Giffard chapel of Boyton church is an oyster shell used as a palette, still containing medieval paint.

Buttermere & Inkpen Hill

START Buttermere, SN8 3RQ,
GR SU338614

DISTANCE 4¼ miles (7km)

SUMMARY Moderate

MAPS OS Landranger 174
Newbury & Wantage; OS Explorer
158 Newbury & Hungerford

WHERE TO EAT AND DRINK
Nothing on the route; The Crown
and Anchor, T01488-668874, in
neighbouring Ham also houses the
Indigo Palace Indian restaurant

This walk covers some of the highest ground in Wiltshire, as well as one of its
quietest valleys.

START From the grass triangle at the northern edge of Buttermere take
the no-through road past the farm and several houses. Once past the
houses continue along the track beyond, bearing slightly left beside the
trees. As you reach the edge of the hillside, a magnificent view opens
up in front of you. Turn right onto the byway (which may be rutted and
muddy in winter) and follow its course along the edge of the ridge. As you
proceed, four counties become visible: Wiltshire in the immediate vicinity,
Berkshire ahead and near left, Hampshire to the right and Oxfordshire to
the distant left.

①   The clump of beech trees on the hillside to your left marks the border
of Wiltshire with Berkshire. As the path descends into a small valley,
look out for Combe Gibbet on the hillside beyond. If you wish to visit it,
continue straight on along the byway.

②   Otherwise, turn sharp right by the clump of six beech trees in the
dip, following the public bridleway sign. Follow the path along the line of
the right-hand hedge, looking to the left for a good view of Walbury Hill.
The path continues between two fields, begins to descend into the valley,
then veers left following the left-hand hedge. It then keeps to the left side
of the beautiful, quiet valley without a building or a road in sight. Follow
the path as it leads between the woodland on the left and the fence on
the right.

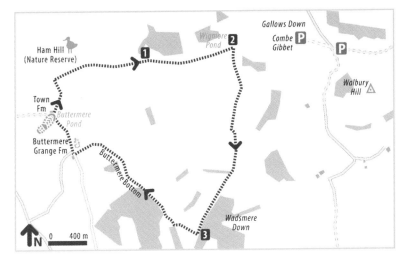

③ Just before it starts to go downhill more steeply, opposite a bridleway sign pointing left into the wood, cross the stile in the right-hand fence. Head straight across the field and down the hill to a gate at the corner of the tree plantation. Go left and continue downhill, bearing right to a farm gate. Make for the chalky track below and turn right, then continue along the right-hand side of the wood and up the valley. Beyond the wood, follow the track as it runs between fences along the valley bottom, then bends round to the left and uphill beneath an avenue of trees. Pass tiny Buttermere church on the left and continue up the road to the T-junction. Turn right past the telephone box and keep straight on back to the grass triangle.

Points of interest

Combe Gibbet, visible from the path, has never been used but is a replica of others that have stood on the same spot. The original gibbet was erected in 1676 following the hanging of the Combe wife-killer, a man from the nearby village of Combe, who killed his shrewish wife and her son so that he could marry his lover. Both husband and mistress were condemned to death and their bodies were displayed on the gibbet erected at the scene of the crime, visible for miles around. The gibbet stands on a Neolithic burial mound, used as a communal grave by the earliest farming communities here.

At 975ft, Walbury Hill is the highest point in the southeast of England and an obvious spot for the ancient hill fort that circles its summit. Walbury Camp is the largest Iron Age hill fort in Berkshire, with a circumference of 1 mile.

START Tollard Royal, SP5 5PP,
GR ST944178 (park by village pond)

DISTANCE 4½ miles (7.5km)

SUMMARY Includes a steep ascent
up a narrow, precipitous path

MAPS OS Landranger 184 Salisbury
& The Plain; OS Explorer 118
Shaftesbury & Cranborne Chase

WHERE TO EAT AND DRINK The
King John Inn, T01725-516207
(serves local game, fish etc.;
children and dogs welcome)

Well-marked tracks along beautiful valleys, then a steep scramble to a ridge
commanding superb views.

START Cross the road to visit Tollard Royal church and get a glimpse of
King John's House behind it, then return to the pond and take the track to
its left, which leads away from the church. At the first fork bear left, and
follow the broad, grassy track that leads along the bottom of the valley.
At the end of this valley, the ground drops away and opens out to left and
right. Go through a gate and follow the track downhill as it bears left, then
go through the gate on the right.

1   Bear right along the next valley floor. Head towards the wooded
slope ahead, joining a stony track. Go through the next gate and continue
along the track beside the wood and past a cottage set in a large garden.
At the next fork, turn left and follow the signed footpath, which forks left
a second time, skirting around a field in the valley bottom. After passing
a clearing to the left, the path starts to climb. Ignore the footpath sign
pointing left, and go straight on along the track.

2   At the foot of the hill, turn left and almost immediately right (with
'Private' signs on either side) up a steeped, signed footpath through the
trees. The narrow path bears to the right and follows the contour of the
steep valley side, eventually leading to a stile in the fence at the top of
the hill.

3   Cross the stile and turn right along the byway. When you can see
the road on your left near the track, continue to follow the byway all the
way back to Tollard Royal and your starting point. As you near the village,
look to your left for a view of Rushmore Lodge on the edge of Cranbourne
Chase and right for a fine view of the church.

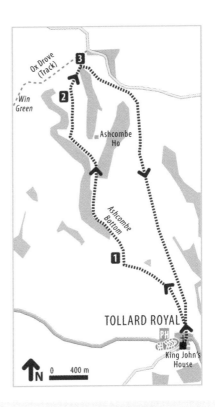

Points of interest

In the nave of Tollard Royal church is a fourteenth-century cross-legged effigy believed to be that of Sir William Payne. It is remarkable in being one of the few examples in which banded mail is represented. There is also a marble monument to General Pitt-Rivers, the archaeologist and ethnologist, who lived at nearby Rushmore Lodge, now a school.

King John's House: King John had a hunting lodge on the site now occupied by this fine Elizabethan manor house. It was later owned by General Pitt-Rivers.

Once a vast forest with a circumference of some 90 miles, Cranbourne Chase was a royal hunting ground from the time of King John to that of James I. By the eighteenth century, however, the forest had become something of a hideaway for poachers, smugglers, outlaws and vagabonds. Disputes and violence arose continually between these and the keepers of the forest, until finally, in 1830, Lord Rivers solved the problem by destroying large parts of the forest altogether, thus reducing it to manageable proportions. Small parts of the ancient woodlands still remain.

Luckington

START Luckington, SN14 6PG,
GR ST833839 (park in Church La)

DISTANCE 4½ miles (7.5km)

SUMMARY Easy walk, mostly
on metalled roads

MAPS OS Landranger 173 Swindon
& Devizes; OS Explorer 168
Stroud, Tetbury & Malmesbury

WHERE TO EAT AND DRINK
The Old Royal Ship Inn,
Luckington, T01666-840222

A short walk through quiet lanes and fields, with good views.

[1]   Walk down Church Rd and turn left just beyond the drive of
Luckington Court to visit the church, then leave the churchyard by a small
gate on the north side. There are stables on your left. Turn right down
the footpath, then bear left before the bridge to walk beside the stream
and pass a ford. Walk past the cottages to a turning on your right over a
second ford. Follow the road for about a mile to a crossroads. Go straight
over and carry on to the next crossroads.

[2]   Turn right down Commonwood La and follow it for about a mile. It
will then bend right, but you keep straight on up a track – there are two
small woods across the fields on your left.

[3]   Opposite the end of the second wood turn right over a stile and,
keeping the hedge on your left, continue to the far corner of the field.
Cross a stile and footbridge into the next field and continue with the
hedge on your left over the next two stiles.

[4]   At the far end of the next field, go through the hedge gap near the
pylon. Cross the field to the house ahead, then walk up the track to a lane.
Cross over to the footpath opposite and go straight on to Luckington
church, now visible ahead. At the Court gates, turn right along the
bridleway, which bends left around Court Farm Cottage, to reach the pub
and the village green.

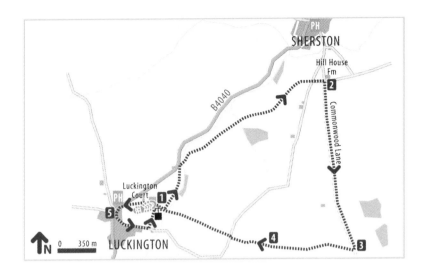

Points of interest

Founded in the twelfth century but much altered, Luckington church forms a picturesque grouping with the adjacent Georgian Luckington Court (not open); the site was a location (as the Bennet family's home, Longbourn) for the BBC's 1995 production of *Pride and Prejudice*.

Holt & Great Chalfield

Start Holt village hall car park, BA14 6RW, GR ST861619

Distance 4½ miles (7km)

Summary Easy walk in fields and woods

Maps OS Landranger 173 Swindon & Devizes; OS Explorer 156 Chippenham & Bradford-on-Avon

Where to eat and drink The Old Ham Tree, Holt, T01225-782581 (pub with garden, dogs welcome); The Tollgate Inn, Holt, T01225-782326 (pub with good restaurant and garden); Glove Factory Studios Café, T01225-784081 (licensed café with garden, open daily for coffee, lunch and tea, dogs welcome)

A walk through open country, linking two beautiful National Trust properties.

Start Turn right out of the car park and follow the road called The Midlands round past the buildings of the old Glove Factory (Beaven's Leather Works, established 1770), now studios. Continue past cottages and a light industrial estate. Notice a pump against a wall on the left with a plaque referring to Holt Spa 1720.

1 When the road bends to the right, cross over to the old cottages opposite and turn left along a track. A kissing gate takes you into a field. Go straight ahead and down through a gap in the hedge, crossing a stream. Bear slightly to the right and at the top of the field go through a kissing gate, over a farm track and through another gate, and past a coppice on your right. Cross the bridge over a stream. You should now see Great Chalfield and Mill Cottages to your left; aim for the top left corner of the field, where a gate leads to a lane. Follow this past Mill Cottages, All Saints church and Great Chalfield Manor.

2 Continue past a sign reading 'Bridleway to Little Chalfield' and pass Home Farm on your left. The land now opens out and the track leads on past Little Chalfield, joining an avenue of beech and horse chestnut trees.

3 At the road ahead turn left and continue past a road coming in from the right signposted to South Wraxall. The road dips down and at the bottom go over a stream and turn right into a field. Follow the hedgerow on the left to the top of the field, where a stile leads into a second field. Continue to follow the hedgerow until on a road at Mirkens Farm.

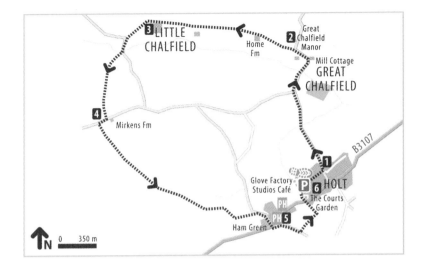

(4) Turn right towards Bradford Leigh but turn left immediately beyond Blackacre Cottage on the left. Go into a field and follow the left hedgerow. The view opens out again and slightly to your right you should see the spire of Christchurch in Bradford-on-Avon. Keep straight on across the field to a stile slightly to the left. Aim for the bottom left corner of the next field; the large building in view straight ahead is the cereals factory at Staverton. Make for the pylon, crossing two stiles, then leave it on your right and follow the right hedgerow. Cross the next field to a stile in the bottom hedgerow into the field beyond. Aim for the bottom left corner. Holt should now be visible ahead. Cross a ditch and follow the hedgerow of the field beyond round two sides to a gap in the corner. Turn left and cross the next field towards the houses, coming out on a road. Turn right and the road will lead you into the village centre, opposite the Tollgate pub.

(5) Cross the main road and walk down the right-hand side of Ham Green, then continue past the parish church of St Katherine. Turn left at a footpath sign, following the church wall, then go through a kissing gate into a field. Go through the stile on the left and turn left to the main road.

(6) Cross the road to the village hall (Reading Rooms) and car park.

Around Dundas Aqueduct

START On A36 about ¼ mile north of junction with Brassknocker Hill, BA2 7BL, GR ST783625 (park in lay-by)

DISTANCE 4½ miles (7km)

SUMMARY Easy walk with one fairly steep climb

MAPS OS Landranger 172 Bristol & Bath, 173 Swindon & Devizes; OS Explorer 155 Bristol & Bath, 156 Chippenham & Bradford-on-Avon

WHERE TO EAT AND DRINK The Fox and Hounds, Farleigh Wick, T01225-863122 (closed Mon); Angelfish Café, Canal Visitor Centre, Brassknocker Hill, T01225-723483 (open daily 10am–5.30pm; walk along the Somerset Coal Canal towpath to reach it)

A walk along the beautiful Limpley Stoke valley, through fields and woods beside the River Avon.

START Walk down to the canal from either end of the lay-by and go left towards the bridge. Cross over and go right on the canal path which leads you over the Dundas Aqueduct, crossing the railway (Bath to south coast) and the River Avon. As the canal turns right, walk to the left of a workshop and over a stile marked 'Public Path'. Continue uphill until a field opens up to the left, then cross this to the top left corner and go over another stile.

1 Turn diagonally right across the next field, then follow a stone-strewn track (quite steep) to Conkwell. Old Bounds Cottage on the left marks the Somerset/Wiltshire boundary. Continue past cottages and turn left at the road junction. Keep on the road, passing a turning to the left, and then look for a stone stile on the left into a field at the end of a wood.

2 Keeping the boundary wall of the wood on your left, go across the top of the next field, then turn left and continue between the wall and a young plantation. As the obvious path turns right, go over a metal gate (unsigned) and cross the field to a stile leading into a field surrounded by woods. Follow the right-hand boundary, turning right at the end and down through a gate. Now go left and through another gate into a wood. Go through the wood and over a gate into a field. Walk on, with the garden of Inwoods on your left, until you reach the main road (A363) at Farleigh Wick. Turn left and pass the Fox and Hounds (or not, as the case may be).

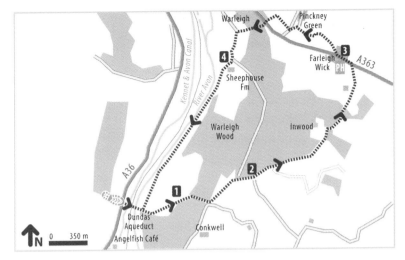

3 Go on for about 100yds and take a footpath on the right to Pinckney Green. The sunken path leads to a gate into a field. Look for the footpath sign in the left-hand fence, then turn right through another kissing gate. Continue up the lane and bear left at the triangle. The cottages to the right were originally quarrymen's cottages. Cross over the next lane and go down a drive opposite, then take the footpath going straight on. It then turns left and, passing some cottages, goes under an arch. There is a bridleway going to the left, but you cross the stone stile straight ahead and walk down through the wood. Cross a track at the bottom and go through a kissing gate into a lane. Turn left and walk to Sheephouse Farm.

4 Go straight on between the buildings until you come to two gates. Take the path on the right, leading down between two fields, and through two further gates to reach the river. Follow on with the river on your right until you see Dundas Aqueduct. Go round the back of the boathouses, over a stile and up steps to the canal path. Turn right to return to the start.

Points of interest

Built in the local Bath stone and completed in 1805, Dundas Aqueduct carries the Kennet and Avon canal over the River Avon and the railway, a total of 150 yards. Notice the entrance to the boat base and moorings on the right. This was the start of the Somerset Coal Canal, in use from 1801 to 1898 and going to Paulton with a branch to Radstock. This first part was dug out and re-opened between 1986 and 1988.

Hilperton & Whaddon

START The Knap, near Hilperton church, BA14 7RJ, GR ST871592 (park near church)

MAPS OS Landranger 173 Swindon & Devizes; OS Explorer 156 Chippenham & Bradford-on-Avon

DISTANCE 4½ miles (6.5km)

SUMMARY Easy walk on field paths

WHERE TO EAT AND DRINK The Lion and Fiddle, Hilperton, T01225-776392

A walk across fields, over the Kennet and Avon Canal and beside the River Avon.

START To the right at the top of The Knap, near the church gate and opposite Hilperton House, you will find a signpost with a bridleway sign pointing along the small lane past the church and a footpath sign pointing to the right. Follow the footpath sign through a kissing gate into a field and bear slightly right, following the right-hand fence past a school, to reach another gate. Cross the field beyond, go through a gateway and over a small stream, then bear right across the next field to a kissing gate. Continue along a path between houses, bearing right when the path forks, to reach a road. Turn left, then, after 50yds, turn right to reach the B3105.

1 Take the right-hand path to the road and cross to reach the track opposite, signed Marsh Farm. Turn down the track, but after 20yds bear right through a gap and cross the field towards a hedge corner. There, go ahead, with the hedge on your right. At the next corner turn left for 20yds, then turn right through a gap and cross a small stream. Go up the right edge of the next field, then walk ahead to reach a hedge and ditch on the far side. Continue across the top of the next field, passing a copse on the right and a lone oak tree, to reach a gate into a lane.

2 Turn left and follow the lane over the Kennet and Avon Canal, and on past some low buildings on the left. Now, just after the road bends left, go over a footbridge and stile on the right and cross the field beyond. Keeping to the right of a house, continue ahead along the left side of two fields to reach the church of St Mary the Virgin, Whaddon. (Here you can shorten the walk by turning right along the track to Whaddon Grove Farm, but you will miss the lovely riverside walk to the old bridge.)

③ Walk a few yards to the left of the church, then turn right over a stile to pass behind it. About 50yds beyond the end of the church wall, as the view opens up, bear left down a grassy bank to a stile, with the River Avon below you on the left, and then ahead to cross an iron bridge over Semington Brook. Bear left across the field beyond to a gate beside the river, near an old railway embankment. Turn right over a double stile and follow the riverbank to reach an old stone packhorse bridge.

④ Do not cross the bridge; instead, turn sharp right and go diagonally across the field towards a group of black-roofed barns. At the far side you will join a track leading to the barns; leaving them on your left go through a gate and follow a metalled track leading up to Whaddon Grove Farm. When the track bends right, near the house, continue straight ahead following a farm track across two fields. When the track bends left, go straight ahead and cross another field to reach the Kennet and Avon Canal again.

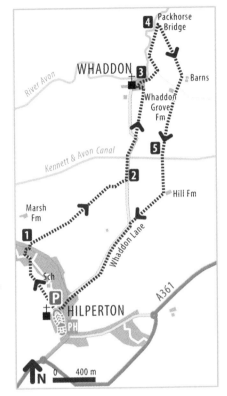

⑤ Cross the bridge over the canal and go up the next field, aiming for a stile about 50yds to the right of Hill Farm. Turn right along the farm drive to reach Whaddon La. Go straight on along the road to Hilperton. At the junction, go on down Church Rd for a further 200yds, then turn right into The Knap (or walk on down Church Rd to reach the Lion and Fiddle pub).

Points of interest

St Mary the Virgin, Whaddon, is a small church with a reconstructed twelfth-century south doorway with a decorated tympanum.
The packhorse bridge, an elegant and well-preserved stone structure, was built c. 1725 to replace an earlier wooden bridge connecting Whaddon with Broughton Gifford.

South Wraxall & Monkton Farleigh

START The Longs Arms, South Wraxall, BA15 2SB, GR ST831648

DISTANCE 4½ miles (7.5km)

SUMMARY Easy walk on grassy rides and fields

MAPS OS Landranger 173 Swindon & Devizes; OS Explorer 156 Chippenham & Bradford-on-Avon

WHERE TO EAT AND DRINK
The Longs Arms, South Wraxall, To1225-864450 (no food on Mon); The Muddy Duck (previously The Kings Arms), Monkton Farleigh, To1225-858705 (pub/restaurant with adaptable, frequently changing seasonal menu, served every day)

A walk linking two old villages, with views of their manor houses.

START Take the road opposite the pub, passing St James's church on your right. Take the first turning to the left and then go right into Green Cl. Cross between fields and go just to the left of some cottages ahead.

1 A stile takes you into a field where you follow the left hedgerow. South Wraxall Manor House is now visible. At the end of the field go over a stile into a lane. Turn left and beyond a farm on the left enter a field via a kissing gate. Go diagonally left across the field and over two stiles near a telegraph pole. Through a copse, a third stile leads into the next field. Cross to a lane. Ahead you will see some tall iron gates and the Manor House at Monkton Farleigh.

2 Go over a stile to the left of the gates and follow a long avenue of trees. About halfway up, go over a stile by an iron gate, then continue until you reach a stone wall and go over a stile by a cottage on the right. Turn left in the lane and at the T-junction turn right up to the church of St Peter.

3 Straight on is the Muddy Duck, should you need refreshment. The walk continues along a path immediately below the church, signposted to Farleigh Wick. Cross over a stile and walk between two fences, then go left through a kissing gate and down steps to a track. Cross over and walk down to the beginning of a hedgerow, then continue with the hedgerow on your left.

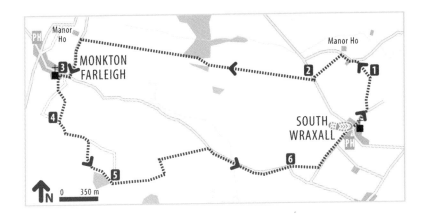

⓸ At the top, through a kissing gate, a grassy track comes from the right, but you turn left to walk around the field edge. Just past the ride marked 'Private', turn left down the side of a field and cross a stile in the middle of the next side. Make for the gap in the hedge ahead, passing a small wood on the right.

⓹ Once through the gap, turn left and follow the hedgerow along the top of two fields, then round to the left and along the edge of two more. A stile by a gate leads into a lane. Turn right and follow the lane until there is a sharp right bend.

⓺ Here, go over a stile immediately to the right of a telegraph pole and cross the field to a lane beyond a gateway. Turn left and follow this lane back to the Longs Arms.

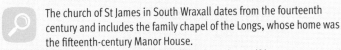

Points of interest

The church of St James in South Wraxall dates from the fourteenth century and includes the family chapel of the Longs, whose home was the fifteenth-century Manor House.
Monkton Farleigh's church of St Peter dates from the twelfth century and has many interesting memorials. The Manor House is the home of the Hobhouse family.

Chute Causeway

START The Cross Keys, Upper
Chute, SP11 9ER, GR SU295538

DISTANCE 4½ miles (7.5km)

SUMMARY Easy

MAPS OS Landrangers 174 Newbury
& Wantage, 185 Winchester &
Basingstoke; OS Explorer 131
Romsey, Andover & Test Valley

WHERE TO EAT AND DRINK The Cross
Keys is currently closed; The Hatchet
Inn, T01264-730229, in Lower Chute
is about a mile away from the route

The route runs along quiet lanes with fine views and well-defined woodland
pathways.

START Walk into the village, leaving The Cross Keys pub on your left. Take
the first turning on the left beside a grass triangle and continue in the
same direction along other small lanes until you reach the church. Still
on the road, walk up the hill for about ½ mile, looking back for a good
view of the church and the rolling countryside behind as you near the top
of the ridge. When you reach a farm on the right, turn left along a path
between two fences. On reaching the road again, turn left. This straight
road along the top of the ridge is Chute Causeway, and the views to both
left and right are superb.

1   Walk along the causeway for about 1 mile until you reach Chantry La,
a wide gravel track on the left, by a signpost for New Zealand Farm. Walk
down the track for about 1 mile, to reach a junction of byways just beyond
the buildings of Rutherfords Stud, with a couple of metal gates straight
ahead.

2   Turn right here on to a bridleway, which descends a little then goes
up the hill, bearing left under trees as it nears the top. Go through the gate
straight ahead and follow the grassy track across the field until it crosses
an ancient earthwork.

3   Follow the course of the earthwork to the left through a gate at the
edge of woodland, and go on through another gate into the wood. Where
the bridleway meets a crossing track, bear left along it.

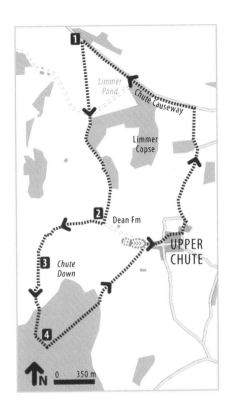

4. Then turn left on another bridleway just before reaching a large clearing on the main forestry road. When you come to the edge of the wood near a cottage, follow the broad track leading to the left of the cottage and up the hill. Go straight on when the farm track bends right, passing a house on your left, to return to the road near the pub.

Points of interest

Chute Causeway follows the course of an old Roman road and joins typically straight roads leading north and south. It is, in fact, part of a whole network of Roman roads that crisscross Wiltshire. Routes between London, Bath, Cirencester and Winchester (all important Roman towns) passed through the county. Nearby Biddesden House is on the site of a Roman villa.

Cherhill to Compton Bassett

START Cherhill church, SN11
8UZ, GR SU038702

DISTANCE 4½ miles (7km)
or 6 miles (10km)

SUMMARY Moderate walk
with some hilly walking

MAPS OS Landranger 173 Swindon
& Devizes; OS Explorer 157
Marlborough & Savernake Forest

WHERE TO EAT AND DRINK The
White Horse, Compton Bassett,
T01249-813118 (nice pub, but
inflexible Sun lunch menu [and may
be fully booked], closed Mon);

The Black Horse, Cherhill, T01249-813365 (on the A4; turn off The Street opposite
The Orchard to reach Middle Lane, and go down the footpath by the postbox)
Lanes, tracks and farmland, with some hilly walking; splendid views, two villages
of character and two fine churches.

START First visit the beautifully kept church and surrounding houses in
Cherhill. Leaving the churchyard, turn left and walk up The Street. On
reaching the top, take the left-hand lane, passing Upper Farm on the right.
Walk straight ahead up the metalled lane marked 'No Through Road'. This
bends round the hillside and soon reaches a group of farm buildings, left.

1 Immediately before the house on the right turn right and follow the
track uphill on the left of the field, with a wood on your left, to a gate at
the end of the wood. Turn left into a sunken track and follow it down the
hillside.

2 When the track forks, take the stony left-hand path and continue
until it reaches a road opposite cottages in Compton Bassett.

3 Turn left here to visit St Swithin's church (tucked away to the left
where the road bends sharply right), which should not be missed. To
extend the walk (and visit the White Horse pub), take the right fork at
2 instead, then turn left into a wider track down to the village street.
Turn right to the pub, and walk on for about ½ mile to see the many
picturesque cottages of Compton Bassett.

4 Continue on to the magnificent late seventeenth-century Manor House, beyond Manor Farm on the left. Walk back through the village to see the church. Retrace your steps to the bridleway opposite the row of red-brick cottages 3 and turn up it.

5 About 100yds up the track there is a small stile, right, at the edge of Home Wood. Cross the stile and walk up the side of the field, with the wood on your right. Go through a small metal gate at the top and continue along the edge of the wood until you reach a wooden gate. Pass through and keep straight ahead across the field towards a house. Pass to the right of this house and gain the lane through double metal gates. Turn right and follow the metalled track, emerging left into a large field at its end. Turn right and descend, passing a small reservoir and down through woods to a road.

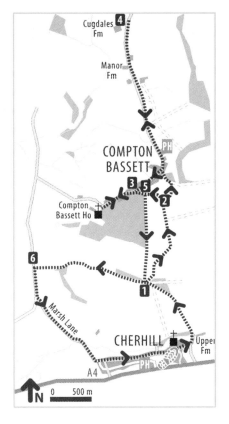

6 Turn left along the road, then left again into Marsh La. Where it bends right in the village turn left into The Street, and return to the church.

Points of interest

Note the fine early fifteenth-century stone rood screen in Compton Bassett church, and the Norman pillars in the north aisle. There is also an interesting barrel vault, with carved bosses.

Ludgershall Castle & Collingbourne Wood

START Car park near Ludgershall
Castle, SP11 9SP, GR SU264509

DISTANCE 5 miles (8km)

SUMMARY Easy

MAPS OS Landranger 184 Salisbury
& The Plain; OS Explorer 131
Romsey, Andover & Test Valley

WHERE TO EAT AND DRINK The
Queen's Head, High St, Ludgershall,
T01264-790334; Café Oasis, High
St, Ludgershall, T01264-792999

A gentle walk, mainly on well-marked paths, through beech woods that are
carpeted with bluebells in spring.

START Follow the road past Ludgershall Castle until it ends by a pair
of cottages and continue through the gate ahead into a field. Turn left
immediately and follow the path along the left-hand fence to a stile. Head
straight on along the gravel track, which leads past Woods Farm and into
Collingbourne Wood. Keep to the track for about 1 mile.

1   As the track drops downhill and veers to the right, continue straight
on up a smaller path between the trees.

2   When you meet the gravelled road approaching from the right, turn
left onto it, then almost immediately turn right along a grassy track, which
continues through the wood. At the end of this track, go through a gate
and continue in the same direction, across a field and down the right-
hand side of a wood. Turn right in the valley bottom, keeping to the right
of the cross fence, and cross the field below the wood to a gate on the far
side. Follow the path winding back into the wood, which soon joins a
larger forest track; turn left along this. Eventually a broad gravel track cuts
across your path; cross this and go straight on, bearing right as you reach
the edge of the wood.

3   Go through the first gateway on the left, and continue in the same
direction along the edge of the field, with the wood to your right.

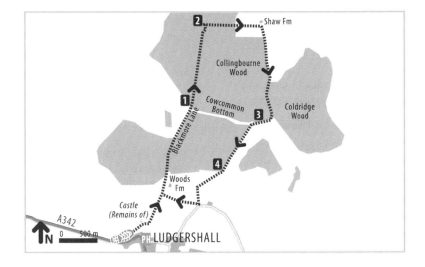

4   When you reach the corner of the wood, turn right through the hedgerow and take the path ahead, which runs between the wood and another hedge on the left. Pass through a wooden gate and follow the line of the left-hand hedge, then bear left through another gate down a track between a small coppice and a hedge on the right. As you reach the road, turn immediately right, down a metalled track leading to Woods Farm. As the track bears right, look for a stile on the left and retrace your steps along the field edge back to the castle.

Points of interest

There is little left of Ludgershall Castle except the grass-covered earthworks and some ruined stone walls. It is thought to have been built at some time during the late eleventh century and was used as a hunting lodge by Henry III in the thirteenth century. The castle fell into decay around the fifteenth and sixteenth centuries. The surrounding ramparts, once fortified with wooden palisades, are extensive enough to give some idea of large and impressive defences.

Collingbourne Wood was probably once part of the great Chute Forest, which stretched from Savernake into Hampshire. A royal forest, it was kept well stocked with deer and in the reign of Henry III red deer were sent to royal favourites or to furnish the royal table.

Gasper Mill

START National Trust car park, Stourhead, BA12 6QF, GR ST778339

DISTANCE 5 miles (8km)

SUMMARY Moderate walk on field paths, tracks and quiet roads

MAPS OS Landranger 183 Yeovil & Frome; OS Explorer 142 Shepton Mallet & Mendip Hills

WHERE TO EAT AND DRINK Spread Eagle Inn, Stourhead, T01747-840587, and National Trust café by car park (both open all day)

A shady woodland walk skirting the Stourhead estate, with occasional vistas across its lakes.

START From the car park, walk to the left of the National Trust shop and café building, past the caravan site and down to the far left corner of the field. Go through a hedge gap here, turn right on the track and cross a stile beside the farm gate. Turn left and cross another stile in the hedge. Cross the field diagonally to a gap in the far left corner.

1 Continue through the next field, with the hedge on your left, towards farm buildings. To the right of these, cross a stile and follow the side of the buildings to reach the farm track. Walk down to the road, passing Bonham Manor. Turn left, with the farmhouse on your left, and almost immediately right into a green lane. Follow the lane to reach a field, and go down its edge with the hedge on your right. Go through a gate by houses and continue on a surfaced road to a crossroads. Go straight over and down a road to the hamlet of White Cross. At a T-junction, turn left by Rose Cottage and go down a steep hill to Vale House. Leave the road here as it bends right, and follow a narrow steep lane down to Fordswater Farm. Fork left at the grass triangle and continue to a stream. This is the stripling River Stour. Follow the river and cross a wooden bridge. Go up a steep, often very muddy, track to the right. As you walk up through these woods you are passing through Pen Pits.

2 Ignore turnings to the right off the main track. At a T-junction turn right in front of a cottage. Where the track splits into three, follow the right, descending track, ignoring all tracks left and right. On reaching level ground and an open field, a track from the left merges with yours, which bears to the right. Continue along it to Gasper Corn Mill, now a private house.

③ As you draw level with its outbuildings, go through a wooden gate immediately to your left and walk close to the hedge along an ill-defined field path. This is Mill La. On reaching another gate, pass through onto a clearly defined track. At a T-junction turn right onto a metalled road and follow this through the tiny hamlet of Gasper. Eventually New Lake comes into view. Continue up to a T-junction and turn left. Ignore a road climbing steeply to the right opposite a telephone kiosk and continue ahead with the lakes below you to the left. After passing under an ornamental stone bridge you reach Stourton. With Stourhead and the Bristol Cross on your left and St Peter's church to your right, go up the road and through a gate on the far side of the Spread Eagle Inn. Go through the inn yard and out through an archway on the left, through the inn car park and back up to the main car park where you started the walk.

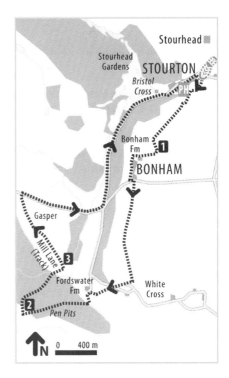

Points of interest

Bonham Manor: the chapel of St Benedict, long since deconsecrated, forms a part of this interesting building. After the Reformation it was a local centre for Catholicism.

The medieval Bristol Cross stands at the entrance to the gardens of Stourhead. It was moved here in 1780.

The hundreds of pits forming the complex of ancient stone quarries known as Pen Pits were in use long before the Norman Conquest. From them greensand stone was excavated to be fashioned into grinding and whetstones.

35 Salisbury Plain & the Lavingtons

START Market Lavington marketplace car park, SN10 4AG, GR SU015542

DISTANCE 5 miles (8km)

SUMMARY Easy walk on clear tracks and roads

MAPS OS Landrangers 173 Swindon & Devizes, 184 Salisbury & The Plain; OS Explorer 130 Salisbury & Stonehenge

WHERE TO EAT AND DRINK
The Bridge Inn, West Lavington, T01380-813213 (closed Mon); The Green Dragon, Market Lavington, T01380-813235

A straightforward walk along part of the Salisbury Plain ridgeway.

START Cross the High St and turn right, then left into White St. This leads up Lavington Hill, steadily ascending the northern scarp of Salisbury Plain.

1 At the top turn right by the Ministry of Defence vedette. There is a metalled road along the line of the ridgeway, but the trackway immediately to the left provides more pleasant walking. Continue for about 2 miles. On reaching the farm buildings at Gores Cross, fork right to reach the main Salisbury to Devizes road.

2 Turn right along the road – looking out for the 'robbers stone' on the right – until you reach a byway on the left in 150yds. Follow this well-defined track, which descends steadily through woodland to an attractive stream with a pond near a cottage. The byway now rises to a junction, from which the lane leading to the right is followed down to West Lavington. On reaching White St, turn right into Rickbarton and cross the main road. Bear right into Rutts La, rising steadily along the metalled road.

3 At the junction with Stibbs Hill, go straight across along a wooded track. On reaching a crossing track, turn left along it and follow the path that leads back to Market Lavington. Turn left when you reach the road to return to the start.

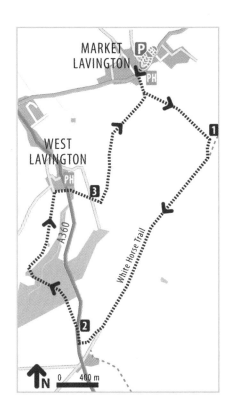

Points of interest

West Lavington is a large village straggling along the Salisbury to Devizes road. The fine clerestoried church holds much of interest.

Market Lavington has been a market town since the thirteenth century. Its farms and buildings along the edge of Salisbury Plain were vacated and demolished when the War Office commandeered the area to extend its firing ranges in 1910.

Around Winterbourne Bassett

START Broad Hinton church car park, SN4 9PS, GR SU105763

DISTANCE 5 miles (8km)

SUMMARY Easy

MAPS OS Landranger 173 Swindon & Devizes; OS Explorer 157 Marlborough & Savernake Forest

WHERE TO EAT AND DRINK The Crown Inn, Broad Hinton, T01793-731302 (lunch Wed–Sat, Sun carvery)

A walk in fields and lanes with wide views across the downland.

START From the parking place, with Broad Hinton church to your right, walk across the field towards the gap between the trees. Go straight on along a broad grassy path that stretches ahead for about 1 mile. (There are good views from here forward and left to the higher ground of the Marlborough Downs.)

[1] When the path reaches Winterbourne Bassett, turn left into a lane and in a few yards the White Horse pub is on the left. A few steps farther on is a signpost to the church across the lane on the right. Follow this, skirting the pond, and the fine setting of the church and manor house may be seen. Continue through the churchyard and church car park back to the village street, turn left and carry on through the village. Follow the quiet lane for about ½ mile.

[2] At the top of a short rise, opposite a turning, take the downhill track on the right marked 'By-Way to Broad Hinton'. There is a stone circle to the right of this track, visible if the grass is short. Just after passing through a stretch of double hedge, watch carefully on the left for a field entrance with a footpath sign on a gatepost. Pass through and make for the farm buildings visible on the far side. Turn right along the track here and in a short distance reach a road. Turn right and proceed for ½ mile to a T-junction with two cottages on the left. Turn left here and follow the road (B4041) for about ½ mile. On the right look for a sign 'Hinton Holsteins'.

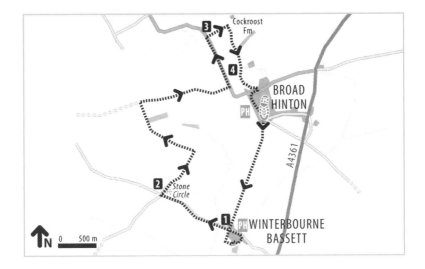

③ Turn right down the track to Cockroost Farm, 200yds ahead. Turn right by the house down a broad farm track. About 100yds before reaching more farm buildings, go through the gate in the right-hand fence and bear left across the field.

④ Go through two further farm gates and cross the cricket field towards Broad Hinton school and village hall. Leave the field by a wooden gate and follow the footpath to the lane. Turn right for a few steps to a T-junction, then turn left down the village street to return to the church.

Points of interest

At Broad Hinton the interesting churchyard has some unusual iron and sarsen tombstones, while the interior of the church contains a fine monument to Sir Thomas Wroughton.

37 Pigs Hill & Marridge Hill

START The Square, Aldbourne
SN8 2DU, GR SU264756

DISTANCE 5 miles (8km)

SUMMARY Moderate

MAPS OS Landranger 174 Newbury
& Wantage; OS Explorer 157
Marlborough & Savernake Forest

WHERE TO EAT AND DRINK
Aldbourne Post Office Café and
Deli, T01672-541353; The Blue
Boar, Aldbourne, T01672-540237

A varied walk among rolling hills, with a couple of fairly steep ascents and easy downhill stretches.

START Leave the village on the Baydon road. A steep climb will take you to the brow of the hill, and after 100yds you will find a footpath sign on the right-hand side of the road, by Baydon Hill Farm. This grassy path runs to the right of the farmhouse then over a stile and downhill, bearing slightly left, towards gallops.

① Duck under the rails, go over another stile, then climb up the left-hand edge of the field to the corner of a tree plantation. Continue uphill at the left side of the wood, until you emerge at a junction with a byway. This area is called Greenhill and there is a beautiful view of Aldbourne behind you. Cross over the byway and carry straight on across a field to the edge of a copse, Greenhill Trees. Keep the hedgerow on your left, winding round to the left and through a crossing hedge, until you come to a wide grassy track with a long gentle descent. At the bottom, turn right onto Pigs Hill. This is a long ascent with Pigs Hill Wood on the left.

② At the top, the track joins another coming in from the left and the surface becomes metalled. This takes you to Marridge Hill, a pretty and quiet little hamlet. Follow the road through Marridge Hill, bearing right at the grassy triangle towards Preston. This is a long descent, with good views on the lower half.

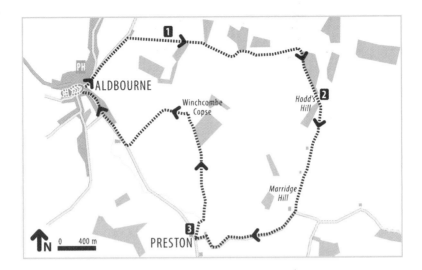

3️⃣ When you reach the bottom of the hill you will pass an ornate Toll Cottage on your left. Turn immediately right along a bridleway, with the brook on your right. After 100yds you cross the brook, which, being fed by springs, is dry from the end of June until springtime. A long climb to the top of Green Hill follows, with Winchcombe Copse on your right. About 200yds past the copse, at a junction, the path going left between fields will take you downhill once more to join the B4192. Turn right along the road (there is a pavement) to return to the centre of Aldbourne.

Wootton Bassett to Greenhill

START The Town Hall, High
St, Wootton Bassett, SN4
7AU, GR SU067825

DISTANCE 5 miles (8km)

SUMMARY Easy

MAPS OS Landranger 173 Swindon
& Devizes; Pathfinder SU 08/18

WHERE TO EAT AND DRINK Emm's
Restaurant, High St, Wootton Bassett,
T0793-854783 (good home-made
lunches and teas); The Town Local,
Station Rd (bottom), Wootton Bassett,
T01793-852480 (good home cooking
served midday and in the evenings);
various local pubs in Wootton Bassett

An easy walk, starting and finishing with some town walking.

1 Cross the High St, turn right and just past Touchdown House turn left down Beamans La. At the bottom turn right for a few yards, then left along a track past a children's playing field into Morestone Rd. At the end, turn left along New Rd, then right to cross the railway bridge.

2 After the bridge, turn right down the track, take a left fork and enter the field on your left over a stile in the corner. Cross the field to a gap between the second and third semi-detached houses opposite. Cross Dunnington Rd and follow a signposted path between houses opposite. Follow the hedge on the left past the light industrial estate until you reach a footbridge over Thunder Brook.

3 Cross the bridge, turn right and aim for a gate and stile in the hedge opposite. Keeping in the same direction, make for the gate onto a road. Cross the road, bearing left to a fingerpost and stile into a field. Cross the field to a gate by a pond and continue across the next field to the gap ahead. Head for the stile in the bottom left-hand corner leading onto a metalled track. Turn right down the track to a stile in the corner by the large gates at the entrance to Lower Greenhill Farm. At the end of the drive take a gate on the left before the main gate and continue on a muddy overgrown track to the next gate and on to the road. Turn left and go uphill to a bridleway on the left just past Upper Greenhill Farm.

4 Follow the path until it emerges into a field, then aim for the start of the hedge to your right and continue past it to the gate in the top right-hand corner of the field.

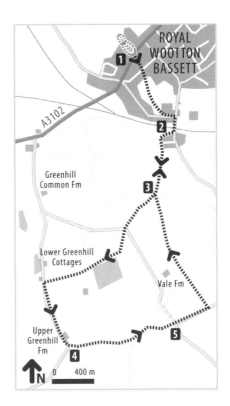

5 Cross the road and continue straight along the road for 300yds, then turn left at a fingerpost and into a field. Cross the field to a double stile a few yards from the left-hand corner. Cross the next field in the same direction, then another stile in the middle of a fence by Vale Farm and on to a small metal gate in the hedge. Cross another stile and roughly follow the line of the hedge on your right to the bridge over Thunder Brook. From this point 3, retrace your steps to Wootton Bassett High St.

Whiteshard Bottom

START Off Stock La from Aldbourne to Axford, SN8 2NU, GR SU238739 (park on verge along no-through road)

DISTANCE 5 miles (8km)

SUMMARY Easy

MAPS OS Landranger 174 Newbury & Wantage; OS Explorer 157 Marlborough & Savernake Forest

WHERE TO EAT AND DRINK Nothing on the route; there are pubs and cafés in Aldbourne, Axford and Ramsbury, all within a couple of miles

A pleasantly varied walk with a long descent to a quiet valley and a sharp ascent.

START Head westward from the junction along the byway, the oldest and most direct road to Marlborough, which proceeds downhill between hedges. A gateway on the left affords a distant view of Martinsell Hill, the highest point on the downs, above Pewsey Vale. The tall hedges are full of tits of all sorts, finches and goldcrests. In the spring look out for violets, bluebells and cowslips. At the bottom of the hill a track comes in from the right, but continue for another 100yds and take a sharp turn along the bridleway to the left beside a small triangular spinney.

1 Our track now goes along a valley between fenced hedges, then alongside great oaks and coppiced hazel. Eventually the path, which can be muddy, becomes a surfaced track through open fields and comes out onto the Axford road.

2 If you have had enough of mud or nettles at this point, turn left along the quiet road. An uphill walk of about 1 mile will bring you past Burney Farm and back to the start. To continue the walk, cross the road and follow the grassy footpath straight ahead, to the left of the hedge, up the edge of a fairly steep arable field. Over the crest of the hill, follow the side of the wood to the bottom right corner of the field.

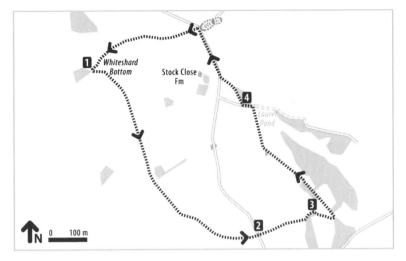

3 Here the track turns right through the wood. On emerging into the next field, turn left and follow the fenced edge beside the wood. Leave the field at the next corner by a short track, which comes out to a byway where you turn left, continuing past New Buildings to join Hilldrop La. Once past the wood there are wide views on the left over the Kennet Valley to the edge of Savernake Forest and thence to Martinsell. Turn left at the road.

4 After about 100yds there is a track on the right that skirts a wood, then crosses some rough grass before coming onto the Axford road. Turn right and follow the road back to the start.

Points of interest

The locality was once part of Aldbourne Chase, which, as part of the Manor of Aldbourne, became royal property under William I. Note the large oaks, dating back to the time when this was a hardwood forest, and the coppiced hazels. These used to be cut back for making hurdles until World War II ended the practice, as sheep were no longer kept in folds.

Middle Hill

START St Aldhelm's church, Bishopstrow, BA12 9HN, GR ST893438

DISTANCE 5 miles (8km)

SUMMARY Moderate

MAPS OS Landranger 184 Salisbury & The Plain; OS Explorer 143 Warminster & Trowbridge

WHERE TO EAT AND DRINK There are no pubs on the route but The Angel Inn T01985-840330 in Heytesbury is open all day, serving food 12–2.30, Mon–Sat; set menu only on Sun, 12–3, booking advised. The village is ¾ mile east of the roundabout marking the junction between the A36 and the B3414.

A fairly strenuous walk across Middle Hill and around ancient earthworks.

START With the church to your right, walk along the road to a metal gate. Go through and follow the path through a kissing gate and over a river bridge to emerge onto the B3414. Cross over, turn left and walk down the footpath until you reach a lane (signed Home Farm B&B) to your right. Turn right here and follow the lane past the farmhouse and adjacent buildings. Go straight on at a junction of paths, over a railway bridge and across a metalled military road. Continue uphill to a junction of paths by a footpath sign near the top of the slope.

1⃝ Turn right and follow the well-defined path across a field to reach an opening leading directly onto another military road. Turn right on the road for a few yards to reach the signed footpath leading through a gap in the left bank and follow it up Middle Hill. Beyond the summit, which is crowned by a tumulus, the path leads down to the left of a small copse.

2⃝ The path continues across a field to a junction of a road and a byway. Walk a short distance along the road, then take the footpath on the right, which leads directly up the short field to a gate. Turn left and follow the clear path that climbs diagonally up the hill, then follows the ramparts of Scratchbury hill fort. Continue to a crossing fence, then go on around the east side of the hill with the fence, running along the top of a valley, on your left. After passing a locked hunting gate, continue to a kissing gate in the fence, go through and walk diagonally right across the field to a gate visible on the skyline.

3⃝ Continue along the grassy path past a group of tumuli until the path forks.

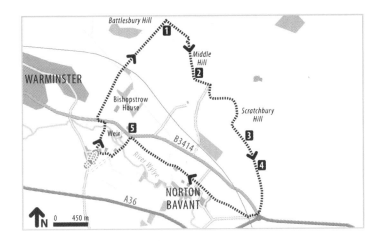

4 Bear right, going downhill to reach the B3414 at its junction with the A36. Cross the B3414 and take the next (unclassified) turning from the roundabout. Immediately after crossing the railway bridge, turn right down a steep, railed footpath. At the bottom, turn left and take a diagonal line across the field towards the nearest house, joining a clear footpath at the hedgerow. By the cottages, climb over a stile onto a metalled road and enter the village of Norton Bavant. Follow the road, ignoring a turning to the left, to a T-junction. Cross to reach a driveway and follow this to another T-junction. Again cross over, into a field and turn left, then right, over a culvert. Follow the field path, crossing back to the right side of the hedge at any of several gaps, until you reach a cottage. Go straight on over a stile into a paddock and continue in the same direction, crossing several stiles, to the top right corner of the field, emerging by the road.

5 Here, turn left into Watery La and follow it over the river. Go straight on when the lane becomes a grassy path beyond the house on the right. Cross a stream, then go right through a kissing gate and follow the path back to St Aldhelm's church.

Points of interest

Middle Hill once overshadowed the ancient settlement of Middleton, of which no trace now exists. The Iron Age hill forts of Battlesbury and Scratchbury, which seemingly buttress the southwestern escarpment of Salisbury Plain, are dominating features of the area. Several paths lead off the main walk route to enable the walker to visit either of the two forts, from which vantage points there are superb views over the Wylye Valley and the Warminster Plain.

Roundway & Heddington

START Consciences La, near
Roundway, SN10 2FQ, GR
SU008633 (park in lay-by)

DISTANCE 5 miles (8km)

SUMMARY Moderate walk
with one fairly steep ascent

MAPS OS Landranger 173 Swindon
& Devizes; OS Explorer 156
Chippenham & Bradford-on-Avon,
157 Marlborough & Savernake Forest

WHERE TO EAT AND DRINK The
Ivy Inn, Heddington, T01380-
859652 (closed Mon)

A varied walk across an interesting and picturesque range of hills, with impressive views.

START Follow the road down the hill then steeply up towards the hamlet of Roundway (or go through the gate opposite the lay-by and turn right to follow the permissive path along the edge of the field). Just before the white gate bearing the village sign, turn left through a kissing gate leading towards Roundway Hill. A defined path now provides the steepest part of the walk. Almost at the top of the hill a roadway is reached. Bear left along this for about ¾ mile.

1 Turn left into the car parking area; from here, a track leads off into the woods, providing a mile-long nature trail circuit with long views to Salisbury Plain. This can be included in the walk if desired. A second track that starts just to the right of the wood (through a gate marked 'Private Property') skirts the edge of a sharp defined bluff with the Oliver's Castle earthwork on the right. Follow this path around the earthwork. On a clear day the views are extensive and impressive.

2 Rejoin the main path by a wooden post and follow it round the bluff and then to the right until in less than ¼ mile it meets a byway, where you turn sharp right.

3 Again in less than ¼ mile look for a footpath sign pointing left. This is the start of a corner-cutting path that crosses a field then falls steeply downhill to join the lane leading from Hill Cottage to Heddington, at a stile. (If the field is too muddy, you can continue along the road to Hill Cottage, then turn sharp left down the lane to Heddington.) Towards the bottom of the lane, the tower of Heddington church comes into

view, and the lane turns sharply right (follow it if you want to detour into Heddington to visit the church or the pub). The route carries on across the front of the farm buildings, then follows the contours around the hillside. After about ½ mile it crosses the Wessex Ridgeway.

④ Over the next crossing track, the path continues slightly to the left and rises a little along a wide terraced way, with views across the Bromham area, noted for its intensive horticulture.

⑤ In just under ½ mile, just after a kissing gate and as the path begins to climb, go over a stile onto a poorly defined path that diverges to the right, leading diagonally downhill towards a hedgerow. Follow this hedge along the lower edge of the fields for just over a mile to reach the Rowde–Roundway road at a farm gate. Turn left along the road to return to the start.

Points of interest

Oliver's Castle is an ancient earthwork. At the battle of Roundway Down (1643) the victorious Royalist cavalry are believed to have pursued remnants of the defeated Parliamentary forces over the edge of Oliver's Castle, with considerable loss of life. Many human remains were later found buried at the foot of the bluff.

The pleasant village of Heddington contains a thatched inn. The church is mainly thirteenth century, with an eighteenth-century decorated organ.

Stanton Fitzwarren to Castle Hill

START Stanton Fitzwarren,
SN6 7RZ, GR SU177904

DISTANCE 5½ miles (9km)

MAPS OS Landranger 173 Swindon
& Devizes; Pathfinder SU 09/19

SUMMARY Easy-moderate

WHERE TO EAT AND DRINK The
Jolly Tar, Hannington, T01793-
762245 (large garden with play area;
good, moderately priced food)

A walk through pleasant farmland and over high ground with good views.

START With Mill La on the left, walk down the main street and out of the village, then follow the footpath on the left signposted to Hannington. Keep to the left hedge and cross the footbridge over a stream and turn right. About 100yds further on follow the left fork of the path between two rows of trees, then, at the farm, turn right down the drive to the road.

1   Turn left and after a few yards take the bridle track on the right next to the Staples Farm entrance. Continue along this track uphill, ignoring the first turning on the left, bearing right instead through Jubilee Copse. As you near the top of the hill, turn left and follow the track. Ignore the left turning to Hannington.

2   About 200yds further on ignore the footpath straight ahead and bear right on a bridle track. This track bears left after a few yards and eventually emerges in Hannington. Turn left down the main street of this pretty village, past the Jolly Tar pub.

3   Just before the next turning on the right, turn left along the narrow path between the cottage gardens and into the field beyond. Go through a metal kissing gate on the other side of the field, and turn right along the fence. Cross a footpath and continue to follow the line of trees, through a hedge and on up to the top of the hill. Locate a gap through the hedge (slightly to your left) to come out on a track.

4   Turn left, then immediately right through a kissing gate. Cross the field and through another gate, down the steps, and follow the footpath ahead. Cross a footbridge, turn right and walk around the field edge, then turn right on a short length of track to Lawn La.

[5] Turn right just around the double bend. Ignore a cross track and walk ahead to farm buildings. Enter a field on the right, then go left through a metal kissing gate into another field.

[6] Head for the oak tree opposite and pass through the gate and up the hill to another gate, then climb up Castle Hill to the fort at the top. Bear slightly left and head for the houses. Turn right along a lane. After a few yards turn left along a footpath that runs alongside the cemetery. The path turns left, then right. At the gate bear right across a field, passing old gun emplacements on your left.

[7] At the road (be aware of traffic) turn left for 300yds, then go through the gap in the hedge on the right. At the bottom of the field cross the bridge and continue down the next field, through the gate and up to the hedge. Go left through a gate and continue in this direction through several fields until you reach the trees at the end of Mill La. Take this back to the start.

Wroughton & Clouts Wood

START The small car park in
Wroughton, SN4 9LW, GR SU145804

DISTANCE 5½ miles(9km)

SUMMARY Moderate

MAPS OS Landranger 173
Swindon & Devizes; OS Explorer
169 Cirencester & Swindon

WHERE TO EAT AND DRINK The
Fox and Hounds, Markham Rd,
Wroughton, T01793-812217 (open
daily 12–11pm; serves food)

A walk along the edge of the downs with good views north.

START From Ellendune car park turn left into Wharf Rd and right at traffic lights into High St. Head up Church Hill, passing two pubs on the right.

[1] On reaching the top of Church Hill take the right fork, signposted Church/Legge House. Pass the church on the right and keep straight ahead, following the path as it descends the hill and joins a meadow path beyond a gate.

[2] On the far side of the meadow turn left into a lane. Walk up the lane, ignoring the signpost on the right to The Kems. As the lane climbs, it takes a right hairpin; carry on up to the left-hand bend.

[3] Turn right here, signposted 'Basset Down'. Continue on the path through several gates and over a metalled track, following the edge of Basset Down Wood to a metalled road. Go straight over and, before the path descends into the woods, keep to the left-hand path with the fence on your right. Follow this path with the wire fence on the right along the edge of a very large field, to where the wood ends (ignoring gates and footpaths to the right).

[4] Go through the metal walking gate at the end of the wood and immediately turn right and go through a metal farm gate. Continue on the path, keeping to the right edge of the field until you reach a metal gate, which is the entrance to the large earthworks of Bincknoll Castle. Retrace your steps back to the metal farm gate and turn left again and go through the metal walking gate (repeat of [4]). Go straight ahead and follow the tufted path which leads across the field with a shallow ditch on the left. In

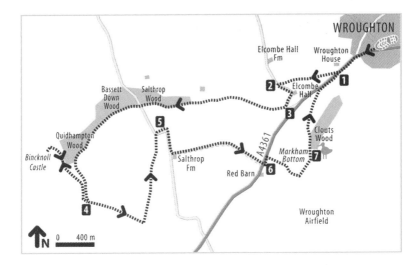

about ½ mile a large corrugated barn is reached by a track. Turn left and follow this track until a second barn is reached. Turn left just before this barn through a field opening and immediately turn right, following the footpath sign with the hedge on your right until you reach a road.

⑤ Turn right into the road, passing two white cottages on the left, and continue until you reach a lane on the left just before a farm. Follow this lane across open downland for about ¾ mile, passing the 208m triangulation point on the left.

⑥ In a short distance you will reach the main A4361. Cross this road very carefully and turn left, passing houses on the right, then immediately turn right, signposted 'Clouts Wood'. Follow the chainlink fence on the right to a metal wishing gate where the fence turns at right angles. Cross the field ahead, veering slightly to the right until you reach a metal wishing gate at the other side of the field. Go through the gate, turn right and follow the path into the valley. Turn left at the valley bottom and continue down the valley, but keeping to the right-hand side until you reach a metal wishing gate at the edge of the woods.

⑦ Go through the gate and follow the left path through the woods, across the stream and through a metal wishing gate, where you take the left-hand path up the valley side following the footpath until you reach the main road. Turn right onto the road and retrace your steps down to the car park.

44 Sugar Hill & Liddington

START A lay-by on the B4192, two miles southeast of Liddington, SN4 0EB, GR SU230786

DISTANCE 5½ miles (9km)

SUMMARY Easy

MAPS OS Landranger 174 Newbury & Wantage; OS Explorers 157 Marlborough & Savernake Forest, 170 Abington, Wantage & Vale of White Horse

WHERE TO EAT AND DRINK
The Village Inn, Bell Lane, Liddington, T01793-790314 (open daily 11.30am-11pm)

An easy walk over high ground with fine views.

START From the lay-by walk to the end of the avenue of trees, then turn left off the road following a wide, grassy track signed 'By-way to Peaks Down'. This is a steep ascent and you will be rewarded by some fine views of Shipley Bottom, which lies behind you.

1 At the top of the hill pass through a metal farm gate and immediately turn left through a single metal walking gate signed 'Liddington Castle/ Bridleway'. Keeping the fence on your left, walk the entire length of the ridge, passing several metal gates signed 'Ridgeway Circular Route'. When the main track bends right towards Manor Farm, continue ahead on the grassy track, following the field edge and into the field which borders the B4192. Follow the field edge until reaching a sign on the left for 'Liddington Castle Circular Walk'.

2 Turn left and cross the B4192. Follow the stony track leading up the hill. At the brow a detour, right, can be taken through a gap in the fence towards a clump of trees. An old gun emplacement can be seen and there are spectacular views of Swindon. Retrace your steps back to the main track and continue up the hill to a metal gate where the track meets the Ridgeway.

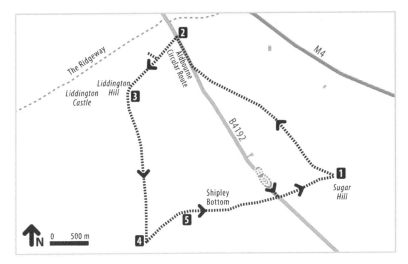

③ Turn half left onto the Ridgeway. A detour right can be taken to view Liddington Castle hill fort from here. To take this detour, proceed on the signed path over a stile and turn left to reach Liddington Castle. The ramparts, trig point and circle of earthworks can all be explored. Retrace your steps back to the Ridgeway ③. Proceed along the Ridgeway for some distance until a signpost is reached on the left, signed Chiseldon to the right.

④ Turn left here and follow a broad grassy track ahead, keeping the new copse of trees on your left. Continue to the end of the copse and then turn right through an opening onto a signed byway.

⑤ Turn left onto the byway and follow the path through Shipley Bottom. You will now see the avenue of trees where you started the walk.

Points of interest

Liddington Castle: the deep ditch and ramparts surrounding the summit of the hill are the remains of one of a string of hill forts on the northern edge of the downs. Its tactical position on the summit of Liddington Hill means that it commands superb views of the surrounding countryside.

Thought to be one of the oldest roads in the country, the Ridgeway runs from Overton Hill, near Avebury, to Ivinghoe Beacon, Buckinghamshire, a distance of some 85 miles.

START Berwick Bassett,
SN4 9NF, GR SU099733

DISTANCE 5½ miles (9km)

SUMMARY Easy

MAPS OS Landranger 173 Swindon
& Devizes; OS Explorer 157
Marlborough & Savernake Forest

WHERE TO EAT AND DRINK The
New Inn, Winterbourne Monkton,
T01672-539240 (closed for
refurbishment at the time of writing)

A gentle walk, mostly on level tracks, with a fine 360-degree view from
Windmill Hill.

START Walk up the lane to the left, passing Berwick House Farm on the
right. After ¼ mile the lane becomes a farm track. Follow this track across
pleasant open farmland for about 1½ miles. When the track eventually
turns right between hedges, continue forwards for about 100yds on a
grassy track towards a hedge and trees. Here the grassy track turns left.

① In a few yards there is a gap between fences in the hedge to the right.
Turn right through this and follow a narrow but well-trodden tree-lined
path, which emerges into a field with a grass track to the left. Follow this
track for about ½ mile, briefly joining a farm track by a small wood, then
continuing between hedges as it gradually rises to higher ground. There
are good views to the right towards Yatesbury, and Lansdowne Memorial
Obelisk (see Walks 15/16) can be seen on the skyline. On gaining the
higher ground a conifer plantation will be visible on the left ahead.

② Turn left here at the signs and walk along the gently descending track
with the plantation on your right.

③ In about ¼ mile, at a well-defined crossroads of farm tracks, turn
right and go straight ahead with a hedge on your right. When you reach
the fence at the end, turn right for 20yds to find a gate leading on to
Windmill Hill.

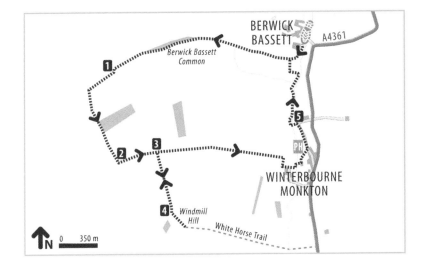

④ After ascending the hill, retrace your steps down to the crossroads ③ and turn right along the broad track, passing a barn, to Winterbourne Monkton. As the track divides, take the lower level left fork and follow it round to the right, then left between houses. When the road bends right towards the church, take the raised path that leads straight ahead. Cross the stream and bear left along a signed grass path running behind gardens to reach the road. Turn left. Follow the lane until it bends right, where you turn left down a no-through road.

⑤ Cross the stream again, then go right on the signposted path to Berwick Bassett, reached in about ½ mile. The path runs alongside the stream, crossing a footbridge, then turns left and right along field edges. When it reaches the lane in Berwick, turn right and a few steps will return you to the village.

Points of interest

Windmill Hill is a famous Neolithic camp. There are several tumuli both within and outside the earthworks, which form a fine vantage point around the whole area towards Avebury and the Pewsey Downs.

Around Broad Hinton

START Broad Hinton church, SN4 9PS, GR SU105763 (car park beside church)

DISTANCE 5½ miles (9km)

SUMMARY Easy walk along village paths and country lanes

MAPS OS Landranger 173 Swindon & Devizes; OS Explorer 157 Marlborough & Savernake Forest

WHERE TO EAT AND DRINK The Crown Inn, Broad Hinton, T01793-731302 (lunch Wed–Sat, Sun carvery)

A walk around attractive villages and farms with distant views of the Marlborough Downs.

START From the parking place, with the church to your right, walk across the field towards the gap in tall beech trees. Turn left along the farm track and keep left following the track in front of Broad Hinton House. On reaching the main road just past the house, turn left for some 100yds. Turn right down Post Office La and in about 150yds take the footpath going left between Sarsen Cottage and Hunter's Moon. The path leads to the right by the gate of Cotsmoor and runs between fences and then by open fields to the right. This soon emerges opposite a large bungalow. Cross the road and follow the path to the left of this. Continue through this small estate of large bungalows and houses (Fortunes Fields), keeping to the path until it ends at a T-junction with a lane.

1 Turn right and walk along the lane for almost ½ mile until a crossroads is reached. Cross the main A4361, passing Weir Farm on the left, and continue along the lane, which reaches the village of Uffcott in about 1 mile. (There are wide views all around to the higher downland of Hackpen Hill and Barbury Castle.) Walk through the quiet and attractive village of Uffcott, keeping to the lane, which turns sharp left after the village. Continue for about ½ mile, when another crossroads will be reached. Cross the main road and continue forwards (signposted 'Salthrop'). Follow this rather busy, bendy lane for about ½ mile.

2 Just before reaching a farm (Salthrop Farm) on the right, turn left down a farm track towards a large corrugated barn. Continue left along the track for about ¼ mile to another similar barn with a waymark beside it. Follow the track forward, at first with a hedge to the right, then straight on over a field. At the top of the field go straight on through the hedge gap to the left of an oak tree.

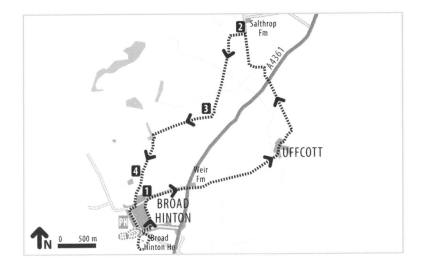

③ Turn right around the end of the hedge onto a grassy track. After about 300yds go through a gateway and continue past a small wood to the conifer plantation ahead. Turn left along the track, and look out for a stile in the right-hand hedge. Cross this and walk diagonally across the field, aiming for the water tower and crossing two more stiles.

④ When you reach another farm track, cross it and continue across the next field to the trees. The footpath passes between two farm pools and over a footbridge, then across another small field. A farm gate in the far corner takes you back into Broad Hinton. Turn right into the lane then left at the T-junction to walk past the post office/village shop and the Crown Inn. To return to the church, continue up the village street to the well, and the church will be seen past the three thatched cottages on the right.

Points of interest

The fine Regency Broad Hinton House has attractive deep eaves and canopies in chinoiserie style over its windows.

47 Lacock & Bowden Park

START National Trust car park, Lacock, SN15 2LW, GR ST917682

DISTANCE 5½ miles (9km)

SUMMARY Easy walk through fields and parkland

MAPS OS Landranger 173 Swindon & Devizes; OS Explorer 156 Chippenham & Bradford-on-Avon

WHERE TO EAT AND DRINK The George Inn, Lacock, T01249 730263 (welcoming pub with open fire and surviving dog-wheel spit); The Bell Inn, Bowden Hill, T01249-730308 (nice pub with large garden)

A walk through a historic village, with great panoramic views over north and west Wiltshire.

START Cross the road from the car park and follow the signed path into Lacock village, with the Abbey on your right. Turn right opposite the Red Lion pub, past the tithe barn, and then right again past the Carpenters Arms to reach the church of St Cyriac. Turn left opposite the church up a no-through road. Two bridges take you over Bide Brook. Walk beside the ford and up the lane past some houses and, at the top, go right then through a kissing gate. Go straight across the field and through another kissing gate to the road. Walk on and then right to Rey bridge over the River Avon.

① Just over the bridge go over a stile on the left and cross the field at half-right aiming for the left end of a stone wall. Go through the squeeze stile, across the road and through another stile. Follow this path round, with a rather fierce-looking wire fence on your left, then go over a double stile into a field. Go left around the field to another double stile into the next field, then follow the hedgerow on the right up a slight bank. Cross another two stiles to reach the Wilts and Berks Canal, now undergoing restoration. Continue along the left bank of the canal, past a brick bridge.

② Cross the canal by a plank bridge and go over a gate into a field. Go over a stile into a small wood and climb up to emerge into a field. Cross to the oak tree at the corner of the opposite hedgerow, then follow the hedge, go through a gap in the field boundary and straight over the next field. Climb over a gate and walk on until you reach a farm road.

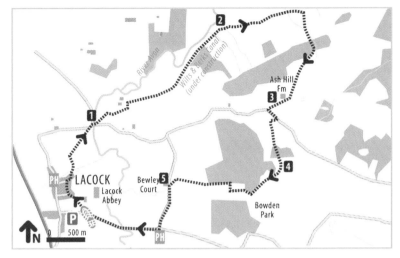

3   Turn right up the road, through the woods, for the long climb up Naish Hill, passing Ash Hill Farm on your right. After the cattle grid and farm entrance, follow the road to a T-junction where you turn left. Just before the first house on the right go over a stile, cross a narrow paddock and go over another stile. Cross the field diagonally to the left and go over two stiles into a wood. Follow a winding path to another stile out of the wood. Walk on with another wood on your right.

4   Over a stile to the right, the path leads down the hill through parkland and you will see Bowden Park on your left, a fine house built in the late eighteenth century. Go around the end of the wood and through a gate into the next field, down to another gate, then cross the large field to the bottom right. Go through a gate on the other side of the field leading out to the road.

5   Turn left and follow the road past Bewley Court and on to a T-junction where the Bell Inn is on your left, but turn right and follow the road back to Lacock.

Points of interest

The picturesque village of Lacock, with Lacock Abbey and many other beautiful buildings, is owned in its entirety by the National Trust.

The 52-mile Wilts and Berks Canal linking the Thames at Abingdon with the Kennet and Avon Canal at Semington was abandoned in 1914. The current restoration project is targeted for completion in 2025.

Somerford Common & Braydon Wood

START Edge of Somerford Common, near Somerwood House, SN15 5DW, GR SU025863 (park beside road just inside wood)

DISTANCE 5½ miles (9km)

SUMMARY Easy, but some bridleways can be muddy

MAPS OS Landranger 173 Swindon & Devizes; OS Explorer 169 Cirencester & Swindon

WHERE TO EAT AND DRINK
There are no pubs on the route; the nearest is The Three Crowns in Brinkworth, T01666-510366

A walk leading through the pleasant farmland and woods of north Wiltshire.

START Walk up the road away from the common towards Penn's Lodge Farm. Opposite the farm entrance turn right onto the broad track and follow it for about a mile, always keeping the hedge on your left. After a while the path leads through a copse (where it may be very muddy) and then broadens out into a grassy track between hedges. Near Somerford Farm follow the track round to the right and turn left onto the road. Proceed along the road, passing Sundays Hill Farm.

1 After the road bends to the left, go through the next gate in the right-hand hedge. Immediately go through the gateway on the left and, bearing right, cross the field, keeping to the left of the oak tree in the middle. Cross the stile in the opposite hedge and go through the gate of Pond Lodge Estate on the other side of the road. Follow the broad track through Braydon Wood, until you come out onto another road.

2 Turn right, passing the water tower, and proceed to the houses just before a T-junction. A bridleway, with a hedge on its left, leads to the right from just before these buildings. Follow it to the left-hand corner of the field, then go through the gate and cross the next field diagonally, heading for Nineteen Acre Wood.

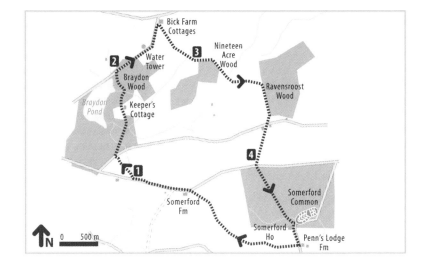

3 Bear slightly left after crossing the stream to reach the corner of the wood. Go through the rickety gate and take the bridleway ahead, which hugs the inside edge of the wood. It leaves the wood at the point where the path bends right for the second time, so go straight on here onto a broad, grassy area. Continue straight on towards Ravensroost Wood, keeping the hedge on your left. Go through the gate into the wood and turn right onto the byway.

4 When you come to a road by a farm, cross and continue along the byway. Cross the next road and follow the byway on the other side leading gently downhill for about a mile through Somerford Common. When you reach another road, turn left to return to your starting point.

49 Castle Combe & Long Dean

START Upper Castle Combe,
SN14 7HH, GR ST845777
(signposted free car park)

DISTANCE 5½ miles (9km)

SUMMARY Easy walk on well-
defined paths and lanes

MAPS OS Landranger 173 Swindon
& Devizes; OS Explorer 156
Chippenham & Bradford-on-Avon

WHERE TO EAT AND DRINK The
White Hart Inn, Ford, T01249-782213
(pub with garden, food served all
day); White Hart, Castle Combe,
T01249-782295 (14th-century pub,
sells ice creams in summer); Castle
Inn, Castle Combe, T01249-783030
(interesting lunchtime bar menu
plus cream teas); Old Rectory
Tearoom, Castle Combe, T01249-
782366 (irregular opening hours)

A walk through quiet wooded valleys and ancient meadowland to a famously picturesque village.

START Walk down the road then go right at a T-junction. At a bend in the road go ahead up a lane signposted 'To Nettleton Shrub', passing Combe House on the right. At the top of the lane take the path past a gate signposted 'Manor House Golf Club'. This runs beside the golf course, following a fence at first, then a stone wall, and leads down to a stile. Do not go over the stile, but follow the path to the right with first a wall then a fence on your left, to emerge on the golf course. The path joins a metalled track leading to a stone bridge over a stream. Leave the track to follow the footpath leading left through woods beside a stream to a tall, stone-surrounded kissing gate at Nettleton Mill House.

1 The path goes to the left between two houses. Go over a stile and continue with the stream to your left. Beware of a wet and muddy patch caused by a spring, and continue to a stone slab bridge. Turn left over this and go up a stony track to reach a lane. Turn left and follow the lane to a road. Turn left again, following the road to a road junction. If you are tired a left turn will take you into Castle Combe village, but our route goes through a gate on the right and takes the footpath left signposted 'Ford 1 mile'.

② Go over a stile and along a path, keeping to the top of the valley until you come to a post indicating the footpath going downhill. Follow the path down, descending steeply through the trees and across a meadow, then over a large stone stile and over a wooden bridge. Go over another stile, cross a field and go through trees to reach a wire fence. Continue along the path to reach a kissing gate. Go through and follow the lane beyond to Ford and the main road. Across the road and down another lane is the White Hart for food and drink.

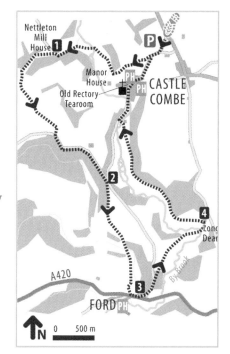

③ Our route goes left at the main road and after about 40yds left again. Shortly, a stile on the right, marked 'Macmillan Way', is taken to a path diagonally across the field and over a stile into trees. Go through a gate and between banks, bearing left into a lane and over a bridge into Long Dean. There used to be two woollen mills here, both now converted to houses.

④ Go left past the post box and Rose Cottage. The track leads towards the sewage works, but at the gate take the path to its right and continue over a stile by a gate, followed by a stone stile. The path gradually descends towards By Brook. There is a gate to go through before a stone bridge takes you over the brook to the road. Turn right into Castle Combe. After a look round this most attractive village, walk up the hill beyond the market cross to the car park.

Points of interest

Castle Combe cannot fail to interest with its market cross, the church of St Andrew, a well-tended memorial and a general peace and tranquillity. It has been used as a location for several films, including *War Horse* (2011).

START Longbridge Deverill
church, BA12 7DL, GR ST867414

DISTANCE 5½ miles (9km)

SUMMARY Easy, sometimes muddy

MAPS OS Landranger 183
Yeovil & Frome; OS Explorer 143
Warminster & Trowbridge

WHERE TO EAT AND DRINK Lake
Shearwater Tea Rooms, T01985-211321
(open Thu–Sun, 10am–5pm); The
George Inn, Longbridge Deverill,
T01985-840396 (open all day)

A pleasant country ramble along clear woodland tracks and field paths.

START Go through a small wooden gate in the corner of the wall to the
right of the lych-gate. Walk across the churchyard and go through a
kissing gate and another gate a little way ahead. Walk diagonally left across
the field to a stile set in the wooden fence. Cross over this stile and climb
up the embankment by overgrown steps to reach the A350. Turn right
and cross over to the side turning, then follow this road to the edge of
woodland. Turn left here and, keeping left, follow the well-defined track
along the edge of the wood until the path forks.

[1]   Take the right-hand path and continue to where another track
merges from the right. Bear left then right, staying on the bridleway that
leads into the wood. At a small clearing by a large beech tree, just before
the bridleway drops downhill, turn left along a grassy track. (Alternatively,
if you wish to visit the tearoom by Shearwater Lake, go straight on down
the hill on the bridleway to the road.) As another track joins from the
right, the path bends right and goes down the hill, passing a one-bar gate,
to reach the road opposite the fishing lake. Turn left and follow the road to
Swancombe Cottage.

[2]   A few yards beyond its drive, a path leads right into the woods and
shortly joins a metalled track. As the track bends to the right, look for
a grassy path running left, parallel with the road. Follow this path until
it brings you back onto the road again. Turn right and walk up the road
until you reach Lower Shute Cottage on the left. Turn left through the
yard in front of the cottage and go through a metal gate. Follow the left-
hand hedge along the edge of this field, then continue on the (sometimes
muddy) track and straight on, still with the hedgerow on your left, until
you reach a gate.

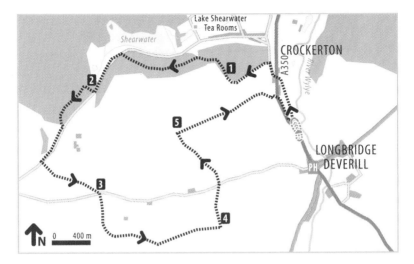

[3] Go through and cross a narrow, metalled road to reach a narrow track between tall hedges opposite. Follow this track down to a gate. Go through and straight on a little to meet a well-defined track. Turn left and walk along this. After passing the house and outbuildings of Rye Hill Farm the track soon broadens out.

[4] When you reach the point where the byway crosses a bridleway, take the narrow path that leads off left, passing a modern bungalow, to a metalled road by Wing Farm. Cross almost directly over the road onto another broad track and walk up this for some distance to a junction with a byway.

[5] Turn right and follow this track, dropping down into a dip (and ignoring the farm track that goes off to the right), until it brings you back out onto the A350. Cross this very busy road, turn right and walk down the footpath until you reach the entrance to Longbridge Deverill church. Turn left and walk down through the churchyard until you reach the lych-gate and the starting point of the walk.

Points of interest

Part of the Longleat Estate, the Shearwater Lake fishing lake is surrounded by picturesque woods with numerous footpaths.
The church at Longbridge Deverill has a small collection of ceremonial armour and an early art nouveau memorial. The Thynne Almshouses, built in 1655, are another interesting feature.

Bishops Cannings & Wansdyke

START Bishops Cannings, SN10 2LD, GR SU036643 (car park at crossroads)

DISTANCE 5½ miles (9km)

SUMMARY Moderate, on well-defined paths and tracks

MAPS OS Landranger 173 Swindon & Devizes; OS Explorer 157 Marlborough & Savernake Forest

WHERE TO EAT AND DRINK The Crown, Bishops Cannings, T01380-860218

A walk combining downland and a short stretch of the Wansdyke with the towpath of the Kennet and Avon Canal.

START Take the metalled road signposted 'Bourton, Easton, No Through Road'. Bear left at the village school (Bourton Rd) and follow the lane to Bourton hamlet. At Bourton take the left of two no-through roads. Fork right shortly and climb steadily until meeting the ridge of Wansdyke near the top of the hill. Behind you, there are ever-expanding views of the Pewsey Vale, across to Salisbury Plain.

1 Turn right through a hunting gate onto the Mid Wilts Way and follow the Wansdyke (*see* Walk 98) earthwork towards Tan Hill. To the left, the Cherhill Monument is visible about 2½ miles away.

2 At the third stile turn right onto a track along the edge of a field, heading for a water tower on the horizon. At the water tower go through the gate and continue down the track, passing strip lynchets to the left. At a field barn, join a farm track bearing right past more farm buildings to reach the Devizes–Pewsey road. Turn right, cross the Kennet and Avon Canal and descend to the towpath on the right.

3 Follow the towpath to a swing bridge, where you cross the canal and pass through a touring caravan site to return to Bishops Cannings. On reaching The Street, turn left between houses into Church Walk to take you through the churchyard of 'the Little Steeple'. Turn right at the main road to reach the car park.

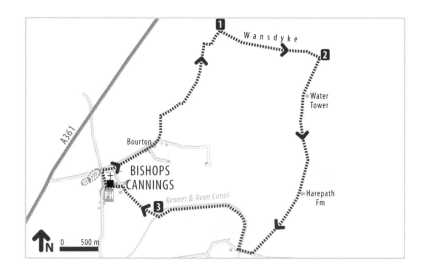

Points of interest

Bishops Cannings is a charming village with one of Wiltshire's finest parish churches, almost entirely Early English. The village is the home of the Wiltshire 'Moonraker' legend. In the nineteenth century villagers were caught by a customs and excise man while raking the pond in the dead of night. They quickly explained they were trying to bring in the large cheese, clearly seen floating out on the surface. The 'zizeman' rode away, laughing at their stupidity – the 'cheese' was only the reflection of the full moon! But the villagers had the last laugh: they had in fact been caught starting to take in a hidden cache of smuggled brandy! Hence the nickname for Wiltshire folk – 'Moonrakers'.

52 Old Sarum & Lower Woodford

START English Heritage car park, Old Sarum, SP1 3SD, GR SU139326

DISTANCE 6 miles (10km)

SUMMARY Easy

MAPS OS Landranger 184 Salisbury & The Plain; OS Explorer 130 Salisbury & Stonehenge

WHERE TO EAT AND DRINK The Wheatsheaf Inn, Lower Woodford, T01722-782203 (food served all day)

A gentle walk along the Woodford Valley, starting from the impressive ramparts of Old Sarum.

START Walk back along the entrance road a short distance, then turn right along a chalky path. Before reaching the main road, turn right again and follow a bridleway signposted to Stratford sub Castle, and at the next gate to Phillips La. At a junction of paths among hedges, bear left downhill to reach the road. Turn right along the roadside footway, passing the church on the right. When you reach the bridge over the river, do not cross, but continue along Phillips La with the manor house on the right, to reach Little Durnford.

1 Opposite the post box, follow a footpath sign through a latched door, along a wide avenue past Home Farm and over a footbridge across the River Avon. Continue to the road, then turn right following the signpost to Amesbury and the Woodfords. Shortly, as the road bends to the right, leave the road opposite a house called 'The Bays' and follow a permissive path along the field edge, which runs parallel to the road then continues along the left side of a wood and straight on to Lower Woodford. At the farm, turn right down the road into the village street.

2 Turn right again (the Wheatsheaf pub is five minutes' walk further down the road) and immediately left into the next driveway. Keep left and follow a narrow path over three footbridges crossing the river. The route continues uphill to reach the road. Turn left along the road for 30yds, then turn acutely right on a footpath beside Salterton Farm. This runs around a field, rising gradually, and bends left to meet a crossing bridleway by a metal gate. Turn right here along a track to Keeper's Cottage.

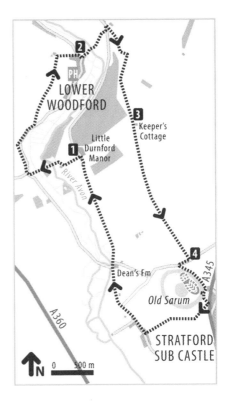

3 Continue straight on to return to the start along a well-defined lane.

4 Just short of Old Sarum, turn right for a short distance on a metalled road before taking a path on the left, which leads round to the Old Sarum access road.

Points of interest

The thatched villages of Lower Woodford and Stratford sub Castle are both very pretty. The church at Stratford sub Castle has a particularly attractive interior.

Old Sarum is the original Salisbury. A prehistoric site, Iron Age hill fort and Roman Sorviodunum, it was later occupied by the Saxons.

53 Rockley

54

START Rockley, SN8 1RT, GR SU162717
(park on road at beginning of village)

DISTANCE 6 miles (10km)
or 5 miles (8km)

SUMMARY Moderate walk
on downland tracks

MAPS OS Landranger 173 Swindon
& Devizes; OS Explorer 157
Marlborough & Savernake Forest

WHERE TO EAT AND DRINK There
are no pubs on the route so best to
bring your own provisions or take
advantage of the many refreshment
opportunities in nearby Marlborough
(2 ½ miles) before or after your walk.

High downland walk on open tracks and paths, through conservation areas and
a nature reserve.

START Set off along the private continuation of the road (a public
bridleway) through the hamlet of Rockley. The route continues up a
broad, downland valley through the Temple Farm estate. The tarmac ends
at Top Temple, but the track continues between the buildings. Follow the
flint track to the head of the valley, where it merges with another coming
in from the right. This is the highest point of the walk.

① Go left along a broad earth track. As it opens into another field, turn
right through the trees and in 50yds go left. This broad, grassy track runs
between hedges and there are numerous sarsen stones piled up along it,
moved off the farmland. On reaching a wood, follow the footpath sign
(marked 'White Horse Trail') round to the right and go straight across a
farm track by a cattle grid.

② Continue along another grassy track between hedges. Go straight on
into the wood and follow the path to the Fyfield Down Nature Reserve.

③ Go through the gate by the signboard and turn right along a
bridleway. Go through a field gate to reach the field of Grey Wethers,
where the scattered sarsen stones look like sheep – wethers – lying in the
grass. Follow the bridleway ahead and walk down the hill past a group of
trees on the right. Turn right on a stony track near the trees, then left after
20yds onto a grassy track, and head towards the left corner of the wood
ahead. From here continue gently downhill. Go through a gate in the right
corner of the field, and leave the nature reserve. Continue across the open

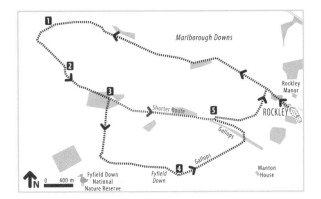

downland, aiming for the gap in the fir trees ahead. Pass two wooden gates and cross the gallops to reach a signpost by a standing stone.

4 Follow the route for Rockley, passing through a gate in a thick hedge and going straight over a road. The route now continues along a wide grass ride. Cross a second road then go slightly to the left of a hedge, and keep the hedge to your right. At the end of the hedge, cross another gallop in a gentle dip. The estate buildings of Manton House can be seen up to the right. Climb out of the dip, cross another gallop and beyond it go left along a third track, dropping gently downhill.

5 At the end of the roadside gallop, before passing a fence, turn right and keep the fence on your left, following it back along a line of beech trees. By a gateway the track passes through the beech trees down into more trees. It broadens out, and takes you down to the lane. Turn right to return to the start.

Alternative route: A shorter walk can easily be arranged by going straight on from the gate at ③. Bear left along the bridleway down a shallow valley, straight back to Rockley.

Points of interest

Fyfield Down Nature Reserve is one of the largest downland tracts containing sarsen stones in Britain, actively conserved and farmed as it has been for many centuries. Here is true, traditional downland, with its attendant flora and fauna. Birds you may see include sparrowhawks, kestrels, long-eared owls, buzzards, red kites and even stone curlews.

Manton House is an old and very large racehorse training establishment, hence the numerous training gallops in the vicinity.

Biddestone & Slaughterford

Start By Biddestone village pond, SN14 7DG, GR ST863735

Distance 6 miles (9.5km)

Summary Moderate walk in fields and woods along quiet lanes

Maps OS Landranger 173 Swindon & Devizes; OS Explorer 156 Chippenham & Bradford-on-Avon

Where to eat and drink The White Horse, Biddestone, T01249-713305 (kitchen closed Mon)

A walk starting in open country and dropping down into the By Brook valley.

Start Walk away from the White Horse pub and, with the pond on your left, go straight on along Church Rd, with the church of St Nicholas on your right. Bear left here along the Butts. When you reach the junction by the cemetery, follow the road to the right of the gate marked 'To Field Barn Farm only'. When the road turns right, go straight on along a footpath marked 'Weavern'.

1️⃣ There are now open views all round; the church tower slightly to the right on the horizon is Colerne. The footpath goes straight on towards a large single tree with a bench beneath it. From here, follow a hedgerow on your left down to a stile and a lane. Turn right and go down the lane until you come to a gate on the left opening onto a bridleway (part of the Macmillan Way), between a wire fence and a hedgerow.

2️⃣ Past the copse on the left, the path crosses a farm track bridging a stream. Bear right (not over the stream) on a path between two wire fences, then cross a footbridge over the main By Brook near a small weir. At the junction of three footpaths, turn sharp right on the path leading steeply up through Monk's Wood.

3️⃣ Crossing a stile, bear right across the field to another stile leading back into the wood. Leave the wood by a third stile and walk along the top of the field, with a large farm shed to your left, to an iron kissing gate. Follow the lane to the right. Turn right at the crossroads along a wooded lane down into Slaughterford, passing a paper mill originally built about 150 years ago. Cross the By Brook and follow the road round to the left through the village to reach St Nicholas church.

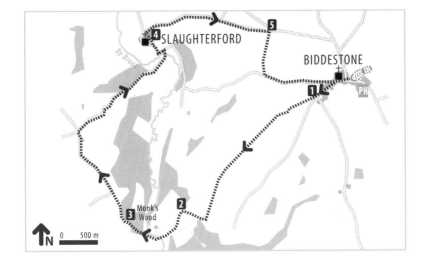

4 Stay on the road, passing a turning to the left (or walk through the churchyard and the field behind to rejoin the road opposite the turning), and start to climb up out of the valley. After about half a mile the road bends to the left and there is a footpath sign on the right. Through the gate, go left around the edge of the field to a stile. Keep going in this direction across the next field to a stile visible in the hedgerow ahead, and on up the hill to meet the lane again to the right of the row of trees.

5 Turn right along the edge of the field, through a gap in the hedge and diagonally across the next field, walking downhill to meet the hedge corner. Around the corner, follow the hedge to a stile into the lane and turn left to Biddestone village pond.

Points of interest

The church of St Nicholas, Biddestone, dates back to the fourteenth century, with box pews. The gallery was put up and used by Slaughterford parishioners after Cromwell destroyed their church. A small church in the middle of a field, St Nicholas, Slaughterford, was rebuilt in 1823 after lying in ruins for 200 years. The thirteenth-century tower is original.

Around Brinkworth

START Edge of Somerford Common, SN15 5DW, GR SU025863 (pull off road just inside wood)

DISTANCE 6 miles (9km)

SUMMARY Easy, but some bridleways can be muddy

MAPS OS Landranger 173 Swindon & Devizes; OS Explorer 169 Cirencester & Swindon

WHERE TO EAT AND DRINK
The Three Crowns, Brinkworth, T0166-510366, is a couple of miles down the road

A mostly flat walk over fields and through woods, which are full of bluebells in May.

START Walk back to the edge of the wood by Somerford House and turn up the byway by the Forestry Commission sign. Climb up through the woods following the track for 1 mile until you reach the lane at the end. Turn left and walk along this quiet lane for the length of two fields on your right.

1 Then turn right through a gate onto a bridleway and follow the left-hand hedge to a gate onto a road. Turn left on the road and walk along to the track on the right leading to Worthy Hill Farm; pass between the house and farm buildings and continue with the hedge on your right to the right-hand corner of Nineteen Acre Wood. Walk on through the wood and turn left at the far side to follow the edge of the wood across its northern end, ignoring the first gate you pass on the right. Leave the wood by a farm gate and make for the gateway opposite at the right-hand side of a short hedge, then cross diagonally to another gate.

2 Go through this and turn right to Bick Farm Cottages, keeping the hedge on your right. Go into the road, turn left and walk along it with the water tower on your right. Continue around the bend and go downhill to look at the pond at Braydon.

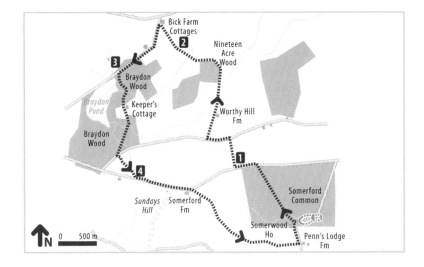

③ Return a few yards to a gate on your right into Pond Lodge Estate and follow the metalled track through Braydon Wood, which is very pretty. Pass the keeper's wooden cottage on your left and continue to a gate onto a lane. Cross over the lane and go over the stile slightly to your left. Cross the field to the left-hand corner with a farm on your right. Go through two gates onto a lane.

④ Turn left and walk past Sundays Hill House and Tanglin Farm gateway to Somerford Farm. At the bend in the road go through the gap ahead and walk along the bridleway (sometimes very muddy) between two hedges. At the end of the wood go through a gate and continue in the same direction, keeping the hedge on your right. The path curves round to the left and ends in a stony track, reaching Penn's Lodge Farm in Stoppers Hill Rd. Turn left to return to the start.

Points of interest

Braydon Wood was once part of the forest that stretched from the Thames Valley to Dorset. Its first mention is in a charter of 796 and Saxon kings hunted here.

Wootton Bassett & Lydiard Tregoze

START Public car park, High
St, Wootton Bassett, SN4
7AX, GR SU067827

DISTANCE 6 miles (9.5km)

SUMMARY Easy

MAPS OS Landranger 173
Swindon & Devizes; OS Explorer
169 Cirencester & Swindon

WHERE TO EAT AND DRINK
Numerous pubs, cafés and takeaways
in Wootton Bassett High St, plus
small café in Lydiard Country Park

A walk across farmland to Lydiard Country Park.

START Leaving the car park, turn left into the High St and walk for about
½ mile until a garage is reached on the other side of the road. Just past the
garage turn right into Marlowe Way and continue to Tennyson Rd on the
right. Just past this, turn left onto a short footpath in front of a bungalow
on the left side of the road leading to the A3102.

1 Cross the road and pass Elmcroft House on your right. Take the next
stile on the right into a field and go past some trees. On reaching the top
of the rise Midge Hall Farm will be ahead. Head across the fields to the
M4 bridge, keeping the farm on your left. Bear right and cross the bridge.

2 Head up the track and, keeping the pylon on your right, bear left to
a gap in the hedge. Go through the gap and cross the field to a stile and
head for Lower Hook Farm. If the crops are too tall, turn left and walk
round the field edge (with the stile on your left). Cross the pair of stiles
separated by a wooden bridge and head towards the road, keeping the
hedge on your right. Cross another pair of stiles/wooden bridge/ditch.
Then cross the field towards the gate/stile which takes you onto the road
in front of the farm. Turn right and head towards a cottage on the left-
hand side of the road. Just before passing the cottage there is a passing
place with a stile on the left.

3 Cross the stile into a fenced footpath bearing round to the right to
a kissing gate. Go through this into Lydiard Country Park and ahead to
the gravelled track, and bear immediately right through a short section of
iron-fenced track. Turn left between an avenue of young trees. Continue
towards a glade. Enter the glade and walk ahead. Signposts will soon be
seen to 'The Mansion', the 'Visitors' Centre', 'Church', and 'Pheasantry'.
Walk down the road to the park exit.

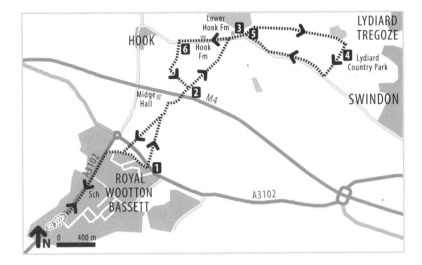

[4] Just before the road, turn right onto a gravelled track. With the road on your left, passing Elm Plantation. Soon after is a kissing gate on the left onto the road. Go past it and continue on the path. Go past a gate onto the road and soon you'll see a stile to the left, taking you out of the park.

[5] Go over this stile and the next one, which takes you onto a track. Directly across the track is a stile into a field (you'll see the cottage that you passed earlier). Cross this stile and head back past the rear of the cottage, where you'll find a stile leading back onto the wide fenced footpath. Cross the stile, turn left and go over the next stile. Pass Lower Hook Farm and continue along the lane, passing Hook Farm, and then a small cemetery.

[6] Just after the cemetery is a small stile on the left; go over this and take the path across this field to a pair of stiles separated by a wooden bridge, then head diagonally across another field to another pair of stiles/ bridge in the right-hand corner. Cross the stiles and walk ahead, keeping the hedge to your left; there will be a stile and bridge in the hedge on your left. Go left across it and head towards the pylon, in front of which is a stile leading to the M4 bridge. Cross the bridge and pass Midge Hall Farm again right, aiming for the garage buildings across the field. At the garage cross the road (A3102) and take the footpath between a bungalow and the Timbervale Guest House. This emerges very shortly in Marlowe Way and thence to Wootton Bassett High St and the start.

58
59

Swindon Old Town

START The Planks long stay car park off the High St, Swindon, SN3 1FJ, GR SU159835 (Alternative start SU149821)

DISTANCE 6 miles (9.5km)

SUMMARY Very easy

MAPS OS Landranger 173 Swindon & Devizes; OS Explorer 169 Cirencester & Swindon

WHERE TO EAT AND DRINK Lots of places in the square formed by High St, Wood St, Devizes Rd and Newport St

A very easy walk through urban woodland, open country and residential areas.

START Cross the High St and walk up Newport St past the mini roundabout. Turn left down the access road into a small industrial area.

1 Turn right and follow the Old Town Railway Path under the bridge. The path continues under another bridge and eventually views over Wichelstow to Wroughton are seen on the left. When the track crosses a bridge, continue ahead for the longer walk but descend to the concrete track for the short walk.

2 The path gradually descends and eventually arrives at the main Swindon–Bristol railway line. Follow the path left along a narrow tarmac lane between fields with the railway on the right. Just before the large farm on the right, go left in the direction of the fingerpost. Walk straight across the middle of this large field to a stile in the fence opposite. Again, go across the next small field and over a footbridge with a stile at either side.

3 Bear slightly left across the next small field to a double stile beneath trees. Following this path should bring you to a stile into a small field and straight ahead is a zigzag path up to Mill La.

4 Turn left towards Waitrose then continue past the store and turn right into Foxham Way, then after about 1,200yds fork left into the road for buses and cyclists only. A short distance before the houses, turn right along a bridle track to the canal and turn left.

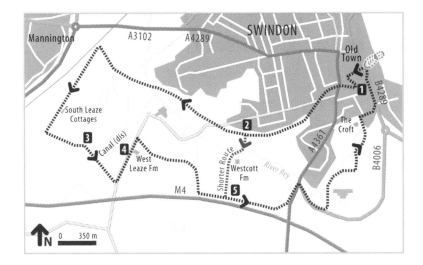

⑤ Walk under the bridge, passing the M4, and continue to the end of the houses then bear right, following the canal under the road bridge. Continue across the field with the hedge and M4 on the right. Go through the hedge to Drove Veterinary Hospital, then up the steps and turn left. Cross multiple crossings including East Wichel Way, then right over three more crossings into Pipers Way. Just before the roundabout bear left at the public footpath fingerpost. On reaching the gravel track bear right, then continue ahead when the track turns left. After a few yards turn left over a bridge, then at a fork bear right uphill. Turn left at the top along a metalled path and bear right at the next fork to pass the car park of the Marriot Hotel on the right. Bear left at the next fork, then up steps to Croft Sports Centre, and continue ahead and out of the gate onto the road (Hesketh Crescent).

⑥ Turn right and, after passing under the bridge, turn left back to the start.

Shorter route: At the bridge ② descend to the concrete track and turn left downhill to the housing estate. Continue in the same direction along Stonehenge Rd and Eyam Rd to the canal, then turn left and follow the directions from ⑤.

60 Clyffe Pypard & Broadtown Hill

START **Clyffe Pypard church,**
SN4 7PY, GR SU074770

DISTANCE **6 miles (9.5km)**

SUMMARY **Moderate**

MAPS **OS Landranger 173 Swindon**
& Devizes; OS Explorer 157
Marlborough & Savernake Forest

WHERE TO EAT AND DRINK
Goddard Arms, Clyffe Pypard,
T01793-731386 (aviation-themed
pub open Fri– Sun only; soup/
sandwiches, cream teas; cash only)

A downland walk along field paths and quiet lanes with some impressive views.

START Leaving the churchyard, bear left through the village street, past the Goddard Arms to the crossroads. Bear right here and walk for about 100yds, then take a lane on the left that bends up the hillside. Just past a farm entrance on the left, go over a stile by the metal gate on the right. Follow this lane, which is metalled, down to another gate.

1 Pass through the gate and follow the grassy track around the hillside. Always keep halfway up the hillside when following this path for about 1 mile, crossing several stiles in pole fences between the fields, with woods to your left and distant views to the right.

2 Pass a small enclosed pond, then go through a farm gate and in about 100yds turn sharp left up a steep track through the trees. Take this path to a metal gate. Pass through and continue to a second gate, then go straight across the field. At the far hedge turn left along the edge of the field, then join a farm track to Bupton Hill Farm. Go through the farmyard into a lane and follow it forwards for about 1 mile. A main road comes in from the left up a steep hill. Bear right here and go forward for about ¼ mile to a signpost.

3 Take the lane to the left for Broad Hinton. Pass a small copse and then a plantation of beech trees. In about ¼ mile the hedge on the left thickens and there is a group of five trees on the right.

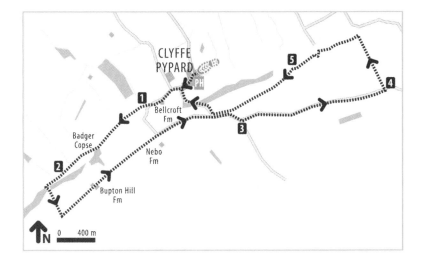

④ About 200yds beyond, just before the lane itself bends right, turn left at the footpath sign. Head straight across the field to reach a wood on the edge of the downs. Turn left here and follow the path along the edge of the fields, above the wooded escarpment, ignoring any paths off to the right. After about ¾ mile a track comes up from the right and merges with your path.

⑤ Follow the now grassy (and possibly overgrown) track forward for about 400yds, the last part along the left side of a hedge. On gaining the road, bear half-right and at the junction ahead take the road right, which descends very steeply through thick beech woods into Clyffe Pypard. Follow the signpost right (marked 'Church') for the pub and the start.

Around Milton Lilbourne

START Milton Lilbourne church,
SN9 5LQ, GR SU190604

DISTANCE 6¼ miles (10km)

SUMMARY Moderate

MAPS OS Landranger 173 Swindon
& Devizes, 174; OS Explorer 130

Salisbury & Stonehenge, 131
Romsey, Andover & Test Valley, 157
Marlborough & Savernake Forest

WHERE TO EAT AND DRINK The
Bruce Arms, Easton Royal, T01672-
810216 (on the B3087 about ½ mile
north of the route at point ④)

A walk on downland above the vale of Pewsey, with superb views.

START Walk on down the main street, past the 'Unsuitable for Motor
Vehicles' sign, until you reach a track on the right, marked as a bridleway
to Fyfield Drove. Continue along this until it crosses a farm track, then
runs past a small wood and bears slightly left along the edge of a large
field. After passing a small lake to the right, turn left at the end of the field
and follow the line of the hedge towards the hillside beyond. You may
just be able to make out the distant shape of a white horse on the slope to
the right.

① In the top corner of the field, pass through the small gap to the
right and follow the narrow path through trees. As the bushes to the left
eventually peter out and the path runs along the edge of a field, head
towards the black wooden barn and the windpump, now visible. Continue
along the path, which at first leads straight on up the hillside, then
curves left on a wide, furrowed track. As you ascend, the views become
increasingly spectacular: first the Vale of Pewsey on the left, then a great
bowl-shaped valley on the right. The path runs in a horseshoe shape
around the top of the bowl. As you reach the far side, look to the right for
the strip lynchets (remains of an ancient, terraced field system) close to
the valley bottom.

② As you continue along the edge of the bowl you will eventually see
on your left a vast long barrow known as the Giant's Grave. Pass to the left
of the barrow to a gate in the fence just beyond. The path now runs across
the fields ahead, eventually reaching a farm road. Turn left and follow the
road until it bends right by a barn, then go straight on along the byway
and continue down the long, gentle hill beyond. At the bottom of the hill
the track meets the end of a minor road. Turn left along it to the next
gateway on the right.

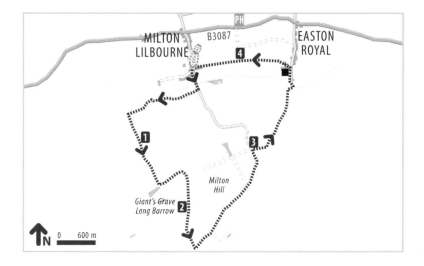

(3) Follow the track along the right-hand edge of the field. At the end of the field, turn left along a path between two fences, and continue downhill until you reach a metalled track. Turn left down this, passing below electricity cables, and follow the track to the right. Turn left at the next junction, crossing a footbridge with white handrails, then walk past several pretty, thatched cottages to Easton Royal church. Take the gravel track to the left just beyond the church and follow the obvious path between gardens to a stile. Continue in the same direction across the field to another stile, then on down the farm track until it turns right. Go straight on over the stile by the gate ahead.

(4) Cross another stile onto a grassy avenue that returns to Milton Lilbourne.

Points of interest

 It is not hard to imagine how ancient burial mounds such as Giant's Grave must have lent credence to myths concerning the existence of giants.

Easton Royal church was built by the Earl of Hertford towards the close of the sixteenth century and has been frequently restored and repaired. There are some slight traces here of a priory of White Canons, disbanded during the Reformation.

62 Wootton Bassett to Bushey Vowley

START Borough Fields pay and display car park (behind Sainsbury's), Wootton Bassett, SN4 7AX, GR SU067827

DISTANCE 6¼ miles (10km)

SUMMARY Easy

MAPS OS Landranger 173 Swindon & Devizes; OS Explorer 169 Cirencester & Swindon

WHERE TO EAT AND DRINK The Woodshaw Inn, Wootton Bassett, T01793-854617; Crown Hotel, High St, Wootton Bassett, T01793-852228

An easy walk, starting and finishing with town walking.

START From the car park walk up the alleyway to the right side of the supermarket entrance and through the shopping mall in the High St. Turn right and continue along the High St past the Town Hall and shops in the direction of Lyneham.

① At the crossroads at the bottom of the hill turn left onto New Rd. Continue along New Rd past traffic bollards and then a left-hand bend until you reach Morstone Rd on the left.

② Turn right here and follow a path leading round the back of new houses to the railway line. Keep to the right at the end of the path and take the steps leading up to the railway bridge. Turn right over the bridge and then immediately right onto a track. After 50yds take a left fork to a metal farm gate.

③ Turn left over the stile to the left of the metal gate, entering into a small field. Go straight ahead towards the houses and find a stile in the gap between the second and third houses. Cross Dunnington Rd and follow the signposted path between the houses opposite to a stile into a field. Follow the path, keeping the hedge on the left, past an industrial estate and then into open countryside until you reach a new metal footbridge on the left. Cross over the bridge and go straight across the field, keeping the hedge on your left, until a metal gate and stile about 50yds from the left-hand corner of the field is reached. Cross the next field and head for the right-hand corner, passing two hunting gates set in a double hedge. Cross over the next field and make for the metal stile,

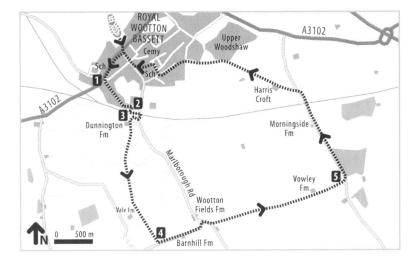

then go over the next field to a double stile over a ditch. In the next field, keeping the hedge on the right, continue to a stile and fingerpost by the road.

4 Turn left and go along the road for about ½ mile to a junction. Turn right for about 150yds to a marked bridleway on the left, just before farm buildings. Follow this public bridleway across the next four fields, keeping the hedge on your right. Upon reaching Vowley Farm, take the footbridge on your right and then immediately turn left, still following the bridleway sign as it passes behind the farm buildings and out onto a metalled track. Turn right here and follow the track to the road.

5 Turn left and continue over the old canal and the railway bridge. Just beyond the railway bridge take the left fork and continue to a roundabout. Cross over the road and head into Bincknoll La, passing Woodshaw Inn on the right. Continue up the hill to the roundabout, using the footpath behind the hedge on the right. Turn left into Noremarsh Rd and head downhill to Washbourne Rd. Turn right and follow Washbourne Rd to a T-junction and then turn left. Cross the road and enter Old Court Playing Field to the right of Noremarsh School gate. Cross the field and turn left along Old Court, passing the Community Centre on your left. Turn right at the road and then at the T-junction right again into the High St. Retrace your steps to Borough Fields car park.

Whitesheet Hill

START National Trust car park, Stourhead, BA12 6QF, GR ST778339

DISTANCE 6½ miles (10.5km)

SUMMARY Moderate walk on well-defined tracks

MAPS OS Landranger 183 Yeovil & Frome; OS Explorer 142 Shepton Mallet & Mendip Hills, 143 Warminster & Trowbridge

WHERE TO EAT AND DRINK Spread Eagle Inn, Stourhead, T01747-840587; National Trust café by car park (both open all day); there are also pubs and cafés in Mere, just off the route

A spectacular chalk downland walk with far-reaching views and impressive earthworks.

START Go out to the road, turn right and walk back to the T-junction with the B3092. Cross over and take a lane almost opposite. Continue to Search Farm, and follow the lane to the right in front of a pair of cottages. As the farm road gives way to a track, stay on this, at first keeping close to a hedge on your right, then continuing across open fields.

① Cross a bridge over the A303 and bear slightly left to a kissing gate. Go through and ascend the steep slope, keeping to the right of an electricity pole. Follow the path along the top of the ridge to a clump of copper beeches planted as a memorial to Sir Winston Churchill. Beyond is the high mound upon which Mere Castle once stood. To climb it, go down to a kissing gate, ignore a set of steps going down to your right and follow the grassy path round to reach a set of steps to the top. Your efforts will be rewarded by superb views, aided by an orientation table identifying various landmarks. Retrace your steps to the point where you came to steps descending to your right. These are now to your left: go down them and follow a descending path down more sets of steps. A footpath to the right goes down into Mere. Continue around the castle mound, then descend more steps to reach a road and houses.

② Turn left to cross another bridge over the A303. Beyond Manor Farm, and just before the next row of cottages, turn right up a chalk track (signed 'Mid Wilts Way') towards a ridge of the downs. Continue through a gate to your left and go on uphill. Follow the edge of the scarp, going through a gate onto a field path as the chalk track continues to the right. When you reach the fence around a tall transmitter aerial, bear right

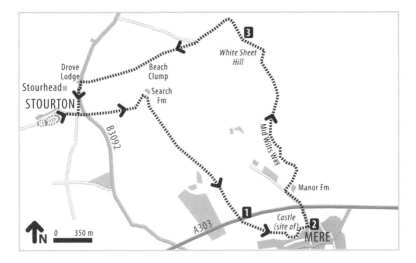

towards a gate with a National Trust sign beside it. Turn left here along a broad chalk track that once formed a section of the Salisbury to West Country coach road.

③ A little further on is an information board about Whitesheet Hill, which you are now crossing, by a stile giving access to the National Trust site. Continue on the track as it descends and turns left. Just beyond is a broad level area on your left used as a car park. Cross to its far corner and take the descending path from there. This leads you down, then up through Beech Clump and finally down to reach the B3092 opposite Drove Lodge. Cross the road, turn left and walk for 25yds to a narrow path leading off through the trees on the right. This soon brings you out by cottages in Stourton village. Turn right to return to the Stourhead car park.

Points of interest

Mere Castle: the castle that used to top the mound was built in 1253 by Richard, Earl of Cornwall to protect the settlement of Mere. No trace of this fortress now remains. On top of the mound there is a memorial to the fallen of the 43rd Welsh Regiment, a replica of one erected outside Caen, Normandy.

Whitesheet Hill is the site of a hill fort, which stood at the southern end. There are many interesting archaeological features, including evidence of a cross-ditch dyke and traces of an enclosed causeway dating from around 3000BC.

Bidcombe Down

START St Michael's church, Brixton Deverill, BA12 7EJ, GR ST863387

DISTANCE 6½ miles (10.5km)

SUMMARY Moderate

MAPS OS Landranger 183 Yeovil & Frome; OS Explorer 143 Warminster & Trowbridge

WHERE TO EAT AND DRINK There are no refreshments on the route, but nearby is The George Inn, Longbridge Deverill, T01985-840396 (open all day)

A scenic but isolated walk on ancient downland tracks with some spectacular views.

START With the church behind you, walk back down the road to its junction with the B3095. Turn right to reach Riversdale Cottage on your left. Here, turn left and walk up a minor road, the metalled surface of which ends by the white Cliff House. Continue ahead on a chalk track, passing farm buildings to the right and going through a gateway. Go on up the track, which climbs beside a steep valley. Just before a line of trees and a fence converging from the left, note a depression in the grass, which is the remains of a dew pond.

1   At the point where the fence ends and the track levels out before descending steeply, turn left along a bridleway to a metal gate. Go through this and follow the line of the fence up the hill. Make for a barn seen ahead shortly, to the right of which there is another gate. Go through and follow distinct vehicle tracks up Cold Kitchen Hill. The large, uncultivated mound to your right is a long barrow. Shortly you reach the OS trig point, which marks the summit of Cold Kitchen Hill at 845ft. The views from here are superb in all directions. Continue to follow the vehicle track to the beacon, where a fence merges from the left. Follow the line of this fence past the head of the next valley and on up the hill. You are now on Bidcombe Down. Continue to follow the fence until it meets a crossing fence, then turn right along this around the edge of the wood, descending the slope a little.

2   Enter the wood by a group of farm gates, following a bridleway signed as the Mid Wilts Way. The path leads through the trees to a gate, then descends more steeply beside a grassy slope to a second gate leading into the wood again.

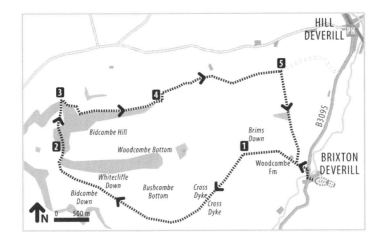

(3) The well-defined track ends at a gate leading into a field. Go through and – leaving the Mid Wilts Way – turn immediately right, on an unsigned path, keeping the edge of Bidcombe Wood on your right. Go down the hill, bearing slightly right to reach two gates. Ignore the wooden gate leading into the wood and go through the metal gate. Skirt the field and continue to follow the edge of the wood for about a mile.

(4) At the end of the field, cross the low fence (the stile has disappeared), turn left and walk to the bottom of the next field. Turn right beyond the hedgerow into a wide grassy track between hedges. Follow this track, passing on your left the buildings and entrance to Rye Hill Farm, where the track narrows then widens out again.

(5) At the point where it crosses a bridleway, turn right. The track soon climbs up through the edge of a wood, after which another track joins it from the right. Continue in the same direction, eventually turning half-right along a farm track, to reach the road up which you previously walked by Cliff House at the start. Turn left and walk down the road to the junction with the B3095. Turn right and walk back over the bridge across the River Wylye, then turn left and walk back to the church.

Points of interest

The modern name of Cold Kitchen Hill may derive from a Celtic term meaning 'the Hill of the Wizard', and numerous archaeological finds suggest that it was the focal point of early settlement in the Deverill Valley. A Neolithic long barrow lies near the summit.

Bishopstone

START Royal Oak pub, Bishopstone, SN6 8PP, GR SU244837

DISTANCE 6½ miles (10.5km); shorter route 3 miles (5km)

SUMMARY Easy

MAPS OS Landranger 174 Newbury & Wantage; Pathfinder SU 27/37 & 28/38

WHERE TO EAT AND DRINK If you park in their car park as suggested, eat at the Royal Oak Pub. Alternatively, pubs nearby are The Rose & Crown at Ashbury (SN6 8NA) or the White Horse at Woolstone (SN7 7QL).

An upland walk with easy gradients along paths/tracks with good, level footing and glorious views to the Marlborough and Hampshire Downs.

START Leaving the Royal Oak, walk back the few yards to the main road and turn left along it, passing the village hall on the right.

① Take the first right onto a narrow lane signed 'Russley Down'. After 75yds, at the last house on the right, turn right onto a gravel drive, signed 'Ridgeway ¾ mile'. Follow this path to a metal wishing gate. The route goes along the side of a small valley with a stream at the bottom and a 6ft-high bank on the left. Walk with the bank on your left to another wishing gate and then into a field. Join a double earth track. The track now curves slightly left into a sheltered, narrow valley, flat-bottomed with steep sides. The path runs through the middle of the valley to a metal wishing gate.

② The path continues up the valley. The path now divides: one route going along the valley bottom, the other along the top right edge. Take either as they merge as the valley opens out. At the far side of a field go through a hunting gate beside a farm gate and signpost, onto the Ridgeway (*). Bear left and continue along an obvious double earth track between fields. After some distance, pass by another track off to the left. A high point is reached with views all around. The grassy track continues unfenced over the brow of the hill and beyond. Go through a metal farm gate ahead into a field with barns on the right and onto a metalled road. Follow the road down a broad, shallow valley. The M4 can be seen ahead, crossing along a hillside ahead of you. Pass over a cattle grid and continue until you come to a narrow tarmac road.

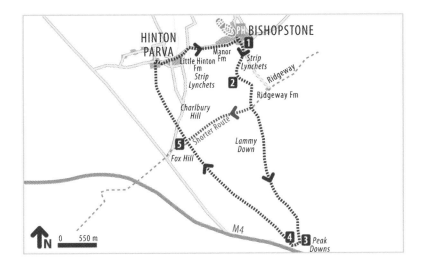

3 Turn right onto the tarmac road and proceed up the hill till you come to the bridge by the M4.

4 Turn right just before the motorway bridge down a short length of tarmac and go through a hunting gate onto the bridlepath with a field on your right, *not* along the M4. The bridlepath becomes a grassy double track and continues straight on. There is a radio mast ahead on Fox Hill and, several hundred yards before you reach it, the path splits. Follow the right-hand path at the end of the wide grass gallops as the track dips down before ascending again to Fox Hill, 790ft. A grassy track continues.

5 At the barn on the right, cross the Ridgeway again (**). Continue straight on where the track bends left downhill to a road, but keep the fence on the right. Go straight on and through a hunting gate, then downhill to a farm gate onto the road. Cross the road and continue straight on down a track with a house on the left signed 'Hinton Parva'. Go through a hunting gate into an area with numerous rubber chip gallops. Keep straight on, crossing these as necessary, and then walk between a double hedge. Go through a hunting gate into 'The Coombes' and keep to the right along the top of this valley. The track gradually drops down the side of the valley into Hinton Parva. Go through a field gate by the village hall car park onto the road.

6   Turn right along the road for 200yds, then take the clearly marked footpath on the left which takes you into the village. At the end of the path, continue straight on passing the church on the left. Where the lane bends sharp right, the footpath goes straight ahead between a cottage and garages. Go past the graveyard and through a wishing gate. Continue on through two fields joined by another wishing gate. Cross the second field and exit by a wishing gate in the right-hand hedgerow and down some steps onto the road. Turn left and follow the road for less than 1 mile into Bishopstone. Pass Bishopstone village pond and return via Cues La to the car.

Shorter route: A very enjoyable walk of approximately half the length is easily achieved by linking the two marks (*) and (**). On reaching the Ridgeway, go right along it until rejoining the main route at Fox Hill. The downs section of the route could be tackled by parking at the Ridgeway notice board at SU233814.

Shaston Drove

START Near Brooklands Farm, on road from Alvediston to Ebbesbourne Wake, SP5 5JS, GR ST985244 (park in lay-by)

DISTANCE 6½ miles (10km)

SUMMARY Easy

MAPS OS Landranger 184 Salisbury & The Plain; OS Explorer 118 Shaftesbury & Cranborne Chase

WHERE TO EAT AND DRINK The Crown, Alvediston, T01722-780335 (just off the route; closed Wed)

Field paths, woodland tracks and an ancient drove road with lovely downland views.

START Cross the road from the lay-by and go through the farm gate signed as a bridleway to Church Bottom. Turn right and keep parallel to the wire fence on your right, following it uphill around the field to reach a kissing gate. Go through and continue walking with the fence on your right, passing through a farm gate and another kissing gate to reach a stile. Cross this and join a well-defined path merging from the left. Turn right and follow this path until a stony cross track is reached.

1 Here, turn left. You are now on the Shaston Drove. Follow the drove road for about 2½ miles, at one point reaching a Y-junction, either fork of which leads back to the main track. Cross over a metalled road under trees, and continue until you reach the second of two conifer plantations.

2 About 100yds further on, turn left onto a footpath going downhill beside a deep ditch. Follow this path down and round to a small wooden gate. Go through the gate and walk down through another gate. Here, the public bridleway runs straight on over the grassy hill, but you can cross the low railed section of fence on the left to enter an area of access land. Turn right and follow the well-defined track running around the valley and down the hill.

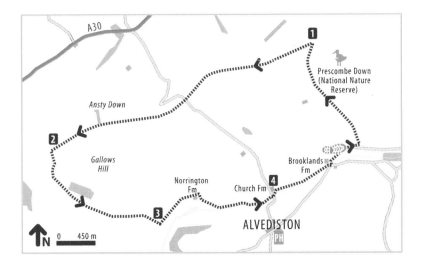

3 When you reach the bridleway running across at the end of the track, turn left towards Norrington Farm, the roof of which can be seen above the trees. Follow the farm road round to the right through the farmyard, then cross a stile by a gate into a field to the left. Keeping the wire fence on your left, follow it until it borders the garden of a cottage. Look for a stile in the fence to your right and cross it into a metalled track. Take the footpath opposite, which leads to a gate into a field. Go through and walk across the small meadow to reach a stile. Cross over the stile onto a metalled road, then walk up the drive almost opposite, which leads to Alvediston church.

4 Halfway up the drive, go through the gate on the right and walk the length of this narrow field to another gate. Go through and walk down a narrow path between cottages until you reach a metalled road. Turn left and follow the road up and round to return to the starting point.

Points of interest

Apart from the superb scenery throughout this walk, there are several tumuli and other earthworks to be identified.

The churchyard of St Mary's, Alvediston, contains the tomb of Sir Anthony Eden, Prime Minister from 1955 to 1957; after his retirement he lived in the manor house near the church.

Bradford-on-Avon & Iford

START Bradford-on-Avon station
car park, BA15 1DF, GR ST824606

DISTANCE 6½ miles (10.5km)

SUMMARY Moderate walk
with one steep section

MAPS OS Landranger 172 Bristol
& Bath, 173 Swindon & Devizes;
OS Explorer 155 Bristol & Bath, 156
Chippenham & Bradford-on-Avon

WHERE TO EAT AND DRINK The
Cross Guns, Avoncliff, T01225-862335
(large terraced garden with views over
river and aqueduct); Blue Cow Café,
Avoncliff (light lunches and afternoon
teas served on lawn; dogs welcome);
The Inn, Freshford, T01225-722250
(attractive pub with sunny garden);
a selection in Bradford-on-Avon

A varied and pretty walk by woods, fields, the rivers Avon and Frome and the
Kennet and Avon Canal.

START This walk can be shortened to 4 miles by starting at Avoncliff, but
parking is limited. Walk to the end of the car park away from the station
and take the path to the river, then turn left under the railway bridge.
With the River Avon on your right, cross a grassed area by Barton Bridge.

1⃞   Passing the Tithe Barn on your left, take the path up the slope to the
Kennet and Avon Canal. Follow the towpath until you come to Avoncliff,
where the canal turns right and crosses the river and railway.

2⃞   Do not cross, but take a path to the right towards the Cross Guns
pub. Turn back to go under the canal and continue past the Blue Bow
Café. Passing Ancliff Sq the path leads on through a kissing gate between
hedgerows, with the river below. Go through a kissing gate and cross a
field following the river, then through a gate into a wood. The path takes
you out into a field by a kissing gate. As you cross this field you come to
the Frome and if you look back you can see where it joins the Avon.

3⃞   The path brings you through a kissing gate at Freshford Bridge. Cross
over and enter a field by another kissing gate. Follow the path and go
right up into the wood and through a kissing gate. Bear left and follow the
path down to the River Frome, left, and another two kissing gates. With
a wire fence on your right, follow on through a gate and out to the road
at Freshford Mill. Go up the road, not over the river, and take the bridle
path on the left by Dunkirk Mill Cottage. This leads to Dunkirk Mill.

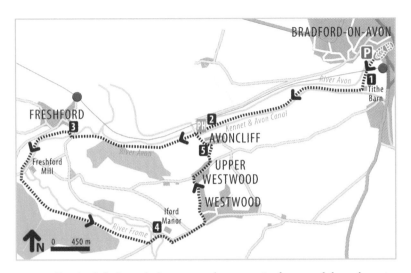

Turning left, the path then goes on between wire fences and through a gate. Bear left, down and over a small stream. Go left about 20yds, then right. Go through a gate and along the narrow field, then through another gate into a wood. Continue, bearing left and down to a stile into a field with the river on your left. Walk the length of this field and go over a stile into a lane at Iford. Turn left and go over a bridge where Britannia is on guard.

4 Turn right at Iford Manor and walk up the steep road to Iford gatehouse and the main road. Turn right and go along until you see a road, The Pastures, on the left through a housing estate. Follow this road and at the end bear left between numbers 45 and 47 along a path to Upper Westwood. Go right and continue to Westwood Park and Nursery.

5 Take the left turn opposite and go past Westwood stone mine to a footpath on the right (opposite Westwood Motors). Go through the stile and down through woods, emerging on a steep road down to Avoncliff, where you can retrace the route along the canal to Bradford-on-Avon. Alternatively, just after leaving Avoncliff on the towpath, take the path to Barton Farm Country Park and follow the riverside back to the car park.

Points of interest

Iford Manor was acquired in 1899 by Harold Peto, who created its Italianate terraced garden (open 2–5pm, Apr–Sept Tue–Thu and weekends, Oct Sun only). Peto also erected the figure of Britannia on the medieval bridge.

North Bradley & West Ashton

START North Bradley church, BA14 0TA, GR ST854548

DISTANCE 6¾ miles (11km)

SUMMARY Easy, mainly level walk

MAPS OS Landrangers 173 Swindon & Devizes, 183 Yeovil & Frome; OS Explorer 143 Warminster & Trowbridge

WHERE TO EAT AND DRINK The Royal Oak, Hawkeridge, T01373-826270 (closed Mon–Tue)

A quiet walk through open countryside and along woodland edges.

START Facing the church, turn left along the road, then, where it bends right, bear left of the tree on the green, past Primrose Cottage, to reach a footpath signed 'Church Lane Nos 51 and 52'. Cross a stile and bear right across two fields. Cross a double stile at the far side and go along the left edge of the next field. Go through a gate at the far side and continue to reach a wide gap in the fence on the left. Go through and bear left to walk along the field edge, with a stream on your left. At the far side, go left over a stile and bridge across a second stile and around a paddock.

① Cross another stile and turn left up to Brook Hall. There, bear left, right, then left again towards two barns. Just past the second barn, turn right and aim for the right edge of a copse ahead. At the far corner of the copse, bear left across a field, aiming for the stile in the opposite hedge. Cross it and go along the edge of two fields to reach the road at Hawkeridge. Cross and go along the road opposite, passing the inn. At the road's end, ignore a path going left, continuing ahead over a stile.

② Maintain direction across two fields, across a track, and two more fields. Go over a footbridge to reach a railway line, and after crossing the line bear left across fields, aiming to the left of Heywood church. Cross a bridge and head towards a bungalow, going between it and a house to reach a road. Turn right to reach a road junction, with the church on your left. Cross the A350, turn left along it for 70yds, then go up the track signed for West Ashton. Go past Woodman's Cottage, on the left, and through the gate of Clanger Farm. Just before the farm buildings, turn right then left through two gates and follow a field edge, then the edge of Clanger Wood. At the end of the field cross the stile in the right-hand corner and bear left back towards the corner of the wood. Cross a footbridge and stile, then at the end of the next field go through a gap on the right across the next field to reach a double stile hidden in the hedge.

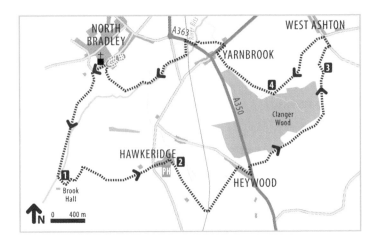

③ Cross and go along the right edge of the next field. Just before the far corner, turn right over a stile and bear slightly left across a field to reach some houses and a road. Turn left for 150yds, then left, through a gate, along a signed path. Go through a second gate, then bear left across a field to reach another gate, down in a small dip. Go through to reach a stile in the hedge at the left edge of a small copse. Go straight across the next field and over a double stile. Now bear right towards a wood.

④ Go over a stile in the corner, then turn right over a footbridge. Turn left along the wood's edge and across a paddock to reach the A350 at Yarnbrook. Turn right for 120yds, then cross the road and go down the track opposite. Go over the stile ahead and bear left across a field. In the opposite corner, turn left over a stile to reach the A363. Cross and turn right. About 20yds after going under the railway, turn left on a path running parallel to the railway, with a pond to your right. Turn right at the field corner; the River Biss is now on your left. Go along the riverbank, passing under a road, to reach the second of two footbridges.

⑤ Here, bear right to reach a stile in the far hedge. Cross and turn right towards North Bradley church. Go over a stile and along an enclosed path to reach a small housing estate. Turn left to reach the main road and turn left again to reach the church.

Points of interest

Dedicated to St Nicholas, North Bradley church has a list of incumbents dating back to 1316. The chalice and paten are fourteenth century.

Bratton & Edington

Sᴛᴀʀᴛ The Duke Hotel, Bratton, BA13 4RW, GR ST915524

Dɪsᴛᴀɴᴄᴇ 6¾ miles (11km)

Sᴜᴍᴍᴀʀʏ Moderate hill walking

Mᴀᴘs OS Landranger 183 Yeovil & Frome, 184 Salisbury & The Plain; OS Explorer 143 Warminster & Trowbridge

Wʜᴇʀᴇ ᴛᴏ ᴇᴀᴛ ᴀɴᴅ ᴅʀɪɴᴋ The Duke Hotel, Bratton, T01380-830242; The Three Daggers, Edington, T01380-830940 (open daily, from 8am for breakfast, with interesting and adaptable menu, ales from the adjacent microbrewery)

A walk with a steep climb, but with magnificent views.

Sᴛᴀʀᴛ Walk along the main road with The Duke on your right and take the second turning on the left (The Butts). At the top, by the old school, bear right. When the road starts to dip take the footpath on the left to St James's church. At the church gate take the path on the right to a kissing gate.

① Don't go through this, but turn right and gradually climb, initially with trees on your left, up a grassy path to the fence at the top. Follow on with the fence on your left, go through a gate and continue between fences. Turn right through a gate and go along a sunken track. Around the head of the valley (known as Combe Bottom), the track eventually meets a road. Cross over and continue round the edge of the earth mound of Bratton Castle Hill Fort. Follow the path until you come to a stone plinth and panorama dial and the Westbury White Horse.

② Continue above the horse and out to the road by the car park. Turn left along the road, then go right by the standing stone and walk towards farm buildings. Turn left round the barn and follow the track for about 1½ miles. All the land to your right belongs to the army. Keep out! Turn right at a road junction towards an army post, where you double back to your left along a grass track.

③ Follow this track, bearing right at a fork, until you come to a barn. Turn right, then left, round the barn. Continue through a gate into a wide grassy area, then bear right to another gate, beyond which go down a gully to a main road (B3098).

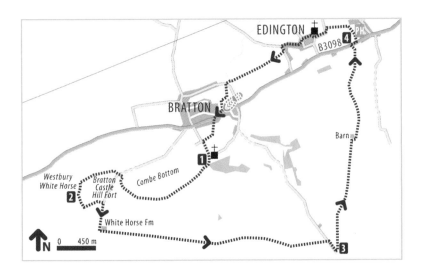

4. Turn right along the road and after about 50yds cross over to a gate on the left. You will see The Three Daggers ahead of you if you need a rest. Otherwise go through the gate and follow the hedgerow on the right until you come to a gate leading onto a road. Turn left, passing houses on your left. Turn left at a road junction and follow the wall on the right to Edington Priory church. Enter the churchyard and take a path to the left and go through a gate. The path leads to a road. Turn left, then first right and right again to walk past the Old Manor Farmhouse on your left. Take the first turning on the left (Greater La), and about 30yds up go through a gate on the right signposted to Bratton. Go through another gate, up a bank and continue with the hedgerow on your right. After a kissing gate, the path leads down to a stream. Turn right, then left across the stream passing in front of a house. Cross the road and follow the path opposite, which leads to the centre of Bratton, the Duke Hotel and the start.

Points of interest

Bratton Castle Hill Fort dates from the Iron Age.

Westbury White Horse is the oldest of many in Wiltshire, but has been re-modelled several times. It was cut in 1778, but there was a much older one on this hill at that time.

The Edington Priory church to St Mary, St Katharine and All Saints dates from 1361. The clock, which has no dial, is one of the oldest working clocks in the country.

Barbury Castle, Burderop Down & Smeathe's Ridge

START Barbury Castle Country Park car park, SN4 oQH, GR SU157761

DISTANCE 7 miles (11km)

SUMMARY Easy to moderate

MAPS OS Landranger 174 Newbury & Wantage; OS Explorers 157 Marlborough & Savernake Forest, 169 Cirencester & Swindon

WHERE TO EAT AND DRINK Nothing along the route. The Inn with the Well, Ogbourne St George, To1672-841445 (¾ mile from the path, returning via Smeathe's Ridge; dog friendly)

A downland walk with stunning views and including the Iron Age hill fort of Barbury Castle and the ancient Ridgeway drovers track.

1 The walk starts at the bridlepath, signposted 'The Ridgeway, To the Hillfort' behind the toilet block. Go through the gate and keep to the left side of the field. Continue through the next gate and straight on, passing the site of the hill fort on your way down the track to the bottom of the hill.

2 Go through the gate and turn right. At the next junction turn right along the byway. When you reach the metalled road (B4005), turn left for 50yds then take the track on the right for ½ mile.

3 Turn right along a track signposted 'Barbury Castle via Burderop Down', keeping the hedge on your left. Pass on the right side of a barn and go uphill to a Millennium Trail post. Turn left and pass three more Millennium Trail posts to a bridleway signpost. Continue straight on between bushes and trees and turn right through a metal gate into a field signed 'Welcome to Herdswick Farm'. Keep to the right edge of the field alongside a line of trees until you reach a concrete road. Turn left along the road for 100yds and take the bridleway uphill on the right. Go through the gate and continue along this track with the fence on the right. The track becomes a hedged lane.

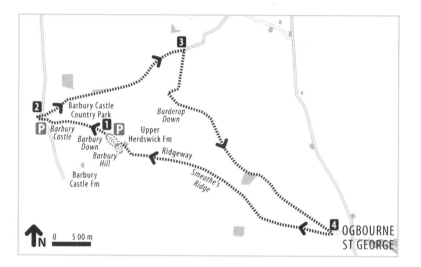

4 Turn right at the metal field gate, signposted the 'Ridgeway' and follow this track along Smeathe's Ridge, going through three more metal gates and passing a seat dedicated to the Secretary of the Ramblers Association, Wiltshire Area. Continue on and go through a wooden gate, and turn right along the Ridgeway, passing Upper Herdswick Farm. Go left through the gate and back to the car park.

All Cannings & Stanton St Bernard

START The triangular road junction in All Cannings, SN10 3NS, GR SU073620

DISTANCE 7 miles (11.5km)

SUMMARY Moderate

MAPS OS Landranger 173 Swindon & Devizes; OS Explorer 157 Marlborough & Savernake Forest

WHERE TO EAT AND DRINK The Kings Arms, All Cannings, T01380-860328 (frequently changing menu, open fires, dogs welcome; closed Mon lunchtimes)

A walk on unspoilt open downland, including a stretch of the ancient Wansdyke.

START Follow the cul-de-sac road towards Townsend. At the edge of the village fork left (signed 'Byway to Woodway Bridge'). Cross the Kennet and Avon Canal at the bridge and go straight on along a lane signposted to the All Cannings Long Barrow. Turn right at the Devizes–Pewsey road, and follow it for about 600yds to Cannings Cross Farm.

① Turn left up the track opposite the farm buildings, then take the right fork, signed as a footpath through a wooden gate, and climb steeply up the end of Cliffords Hill with a fence on your right. Follow the broad grassy ridge until the path bends to the left and descends slightly before rising to Rybury Camp.

② After exploring the earthworks, drop steeply to a farm gate and join a well-marked path, bearing right and going gradually uphill. Near the top, the path goes through a gate and continues over the hill in the same direction until it meets the ancient Wansdyke (see Walk 51). Turn right along the dyke and follow it for nearly 1½ miles. There are fine views to the north, and Silbury Hill is visible.

③ At a roadway, turn sharp right and descend towards Stanton St Bernard. Above and to the left is a slope much favoured by hang gliders at weekends. Just after passing the drive to Hill Barn, bear left, staying on the farm track, then carry straight on at the next farm building. Cross the Devizes–Pewsey road and walk down the side road opposite into Stanton St Bernard. Go straight ahead at Church Farm when the road turns left,

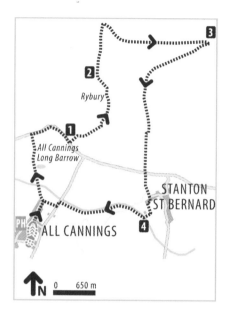

and follow the lane round to the right. By the Pewsey Vale Riding Centre turn left onto a broad track leading to the Kennet and Avon Canal.

(4)   Cross the bridge and go through the gate on the right to reach the towpath. Just before the bridge carrying the road into All Cannings, turn left off the towpath through the car park, then cross the road and follow the byway opposite, along the edge of a field. Turn left down the Townsend road to return to the start.

Points of interest

All Cannings Long Barrow was built from local sarsen stones and completed in 2014. It is the first long barrow to be constructed in Wiltshire for 5,000 years. Niches inside are designed to hold cremated remains.

Rybury Camp is an Iron Age hill fort with a prominent ditch and banking.

Stanton St Bernard is a rather isolated village. The church, with the exception of the Perpendicular tower, dates from 1833.

All Cannings contains thatched houses and a sizeable church – Norman, Early English, Perpendicular, Victorian. There is a village store.

Bradenstoke & Great Wood

START St Mary the Virgin church, Bradenstoke, SN15 4EL, GR SU001794

DISTANCE 7 miles (11.5km)

SUMMARY Easy

MAPS OS Landranger 173 Swindon & Devizes; OS Explorer 169 Cirencester & Swindon

WHERE TO EAT AND DRINK The Cross Keys, Bradenstoke, T01249-892200

Hilly, wooded country with extensive views towards the Bristol Channel.

START Facing the church, turn left along the road through the village. Shortly after a right bend, with St Mary's Close on the right, turn left into Boundary Close. Almost immediately cross Barton Close to a path signposted to The Tops and other houses. Follow it between the houses and continue between fences, with good views to the left. Continue past bungalows on the right to reach the B4069. Cross, with care, and turn right for 20yds. Now, just past a house (7 The Banks), turn left up steps and along an enclosed path. After passing a bungalow on the right, continue along the left edge of a long field. At the far end, follow the hedge round to the right for 20yds, then go through a squeeze stile.

① Turn left, towards the gate at the top of another path coming up the hill, but do not go through; instead, follow the field edge to its right then walk diagonally right, across the open access land of Bailey's Hill, to a stile.

② Cross it and continue along the right-hand edge of the next field to reach a road. Cross the road and go over the stile. Head across the middle of the field and cross another stile at the far side. Maintain direction across the next field; there is a reservoir to your right among trees.

③ Go through the right-hand gap in the hedge and bear right across fields, down to a lane. Turn left. Pass the first footpath sign on your right and, after a further 20yds, turn right through the gates of Tor Lane Farm. Follow the track round to the right of the farmhouse and across the railway. Stay on the track through the hedgerow, crossing another track leading to a barn and past the first paddock, then turn right on a grassy path.

④ Going diagonally left, climb the hill to reach a hedge corner and go on with the hedge on your left. At the next corner, go down a steep track through the trees, and follow it round to the right for 30yds, then look for a farm gate to the left (the path may be overgrown here). Go through

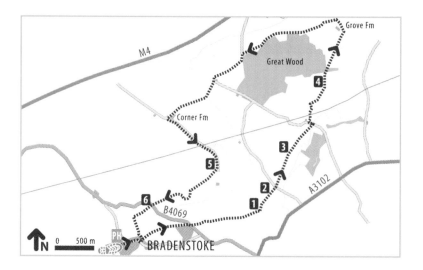

the gate into an uncultivated meadow, with Great Wood on your left. Walk down the field, heading to the right of Grove Farm. Go through the wooden gate into the next field and turn left along its edge, with the farm on your left. At a hedge corner, bear slightly right across the field to cross the farm track near the road. Cross the track and go along another track, just opposite. Pass Blunt's Cottages and continue through a hedge gap ahead and along the middle of a long, narrow field. Great Wood is over to your left. Cross the next field to reach another corner of the wood, then go through another hedge gap and turn left along the wood edge. Cross a stile and footbridge and cross the next field to reach a stile by a barn at Gable End Farm. Go through the farmyard and turn left along a road for about a mile. Where the road turns right, at Corner Farm, turn left along Sodom La. Follow the lane under the railway, then over a disused canal.

⑤ Just after passing a house on the left, turn right over a footbridge and stile in the hedge. Bear left diagonally up the field and go over the double stile at the far side. The right of way runs to the right of Park Farm, but if this is obstructed by paddock fencing, aim to the left of the farm and join a gravel track running into the farmyard. Cross it and turn left onto the farm track to reach the B4069.

⑥ Cross the road to a stile a few yards to the right and walk up the field to a hedge, then turn right along it to a gate at the end on the left. Go through this and follow the farm track across the valley to return to Bradenstoke village street. Turn right to return to the church.

Ancient Wiltshire

START National Trust car park,
Avebury, SN8 1RE, GR SU099696

DISTANCE 7 miles (11km)

SUMMARY Moderate
walk on clear paths

MAPS OS Landranger 173 Swindon
& Devizes; OS Explorer 157
Marlborough & Savernake Forest

WHERE TO EAT AND DRINK
The Red Lion, Avebury, T01672-
539266 (open all day)

A downland walk visiting the huge stone circle at Avebury and other important
archaeological sites.

START Leave the car park by the path to the village if you wish to visit the
Manor House and church first, both very worthwhile. Otherwise, cross the
A4361 and turn right for a few yards to a farm entrance. Turn down the
track, then go through the gate to the right onto a footpath leading around
Silbury Hill (there is no public access to the hill itself). Go through two
gates by the footbridge.

1   Continue, over two stiles and through another gate, following the
White Horse Trail. Cross the A4 road to the cottage on the left, and go
down the footpath signposted to West Kennet Long Barrow.

2   Just after the path swings left, turn right uphill to reach the barrow.
Retrace your steps from the barrow to rejoin the main path.

3   Turn right here and follow the left-hand side of the field to a gate;
go through and along a farm track. Cross the road and go through a gate.
Follow the right-hand side of the field, going over a stile among trees at
a crossing track. Go left and right to follow the bridleway leading up the
hill. At a lane, turn left and descend to East Kennet. At a T-junction turn
right. After 100yds, just after a road sign indicating the next T-junction,
turn left along an alley beside a house. Turn left onto a road and follow the
left fork to a bridge over the River Kennet. Cross the river and follow the
bridleway round to the left, then right up the byway to pass alongside the
Sanctuary.

4   Cross the main road and walk along the wide grass path, the
Ridgeway, for nearly 2 miles.

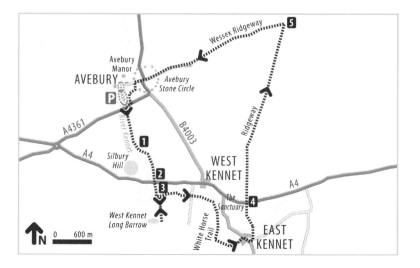

⑤ At the crossing of tracks, turn left following the sign 'Avebury 1½ miles'. Where the track becomes a lane, continue straight ahead through the Avebury stone circle and across the main road back into the village.

Points of interest

Avebury Manor was once the home of Alexander Keiller, who excavated and re-erected much of the stone circle. The house and museum are owned by the National Trust and are open daily 11am–5pm Apr–Oct, 11am–4pm Nov–Mar.

Silbury Hill is the largest manmade mound in Europe, standing over 130ft high and covering 5 acres. It was built, in four phases, from about 4,500 years ago, but its use is a mystery.

West Kennet Long Barrow, an enormous Neolithic burial chamber, was constructed about 2,500BC. Over 100yds long, it has an entrance of huge sarsen stones.

The Sanctuary consists of two circles of sarsen stones erected by Bronze Age people, marking a circular building, perhaps a temple. A 50ft-wide avenue of standing stones once led, for more than 1 mile, from Avebury to the Sanctuary, and many of these can still be seen along the side of the B4003 road connecting Avebury with West Kennet.

Avebury Stone Circle, the largest in Europe, is a huge and impressive monument. One stone of the inner Great Circle weighs over 40 tons.

Around Crofton

START By the canal bridge on the road from Burbage to Durley, SN8 3AY, GR SU235633

DISTANCE 7 miles (11km)

SUMMARY Easy

MAPS OS Landranger 174 Newbury & Wantage; OS Explorer 157 Marlborough & Savernake Forest

WHERE TO EAT AND DRINK Engineman's Rest Café, Crofton Pumping Station, is open daily Easter–Oct; T01672-870300

A basically level walk including woodland, open parkland and interesting canal features.

START Set off up the road to Durley, looking out for a signpost on the right in about ½ mile to 'St Katharine's – 1¾ miles'. Follow the line indicated, crossing a field towards a patch of woodland. Go through this woodland, over several stiles and an approach road to Tottenham House, to reach a large field.

1 Make for the central of three clumps of trees and reach another stile on the far side of the field. The way now continues through woodland to reach St Katharine's church. Just beyond the church follow the signpost towards Stokke along the southern fringe of Bedwyn Common, passing a 'No Through Road' sign. At a junction of paths by a group of cottages, bear right up a rise and turn right again on reaching another house. Follow the metalled road until it ends at the front gate of a large house, where you continue straight on along a less well-defined path. Descend a little and then turn left along a crossing track.

2 This is Hatchet La, which runs fairly straight in a depression between open fields, to reach the road at the western edge of Great Bedwyn village (*see* Walk 9). Go straight on, crossing the railway and the Kennet and Avon canal (*see* Walk 11), then turn right through the car park to reach the canal towpath.

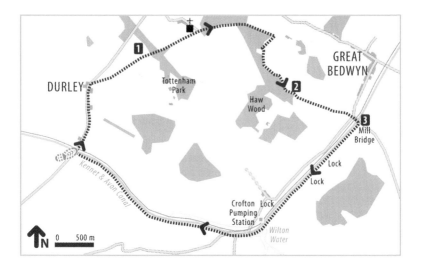

③ Turn left and walk for just over 3 miles to return to the start. Along the canal you will see abundant water fowl, the restored canal locks rising to the summit level, the Crofton Pumping Station (*see* Walk 11), the abutments of skew bridges that once carried the Midland and South Western Junction Railway over the canal, and the Bruce Tunnel, with its plaque over the eastern portal. As there is no towpath through the tunnel, the track angles up to the left just before the tunnel entrance.

Points of interest

St Katharine's church was designed by Wyatt and built in 1861 but is now considerably altered. There's a notable churchyard with firs, cypresses and a ha-ha.

Crofton Pumping Station – *see* Walk 11.

Broad Chalke & the Ebble Valley

START United Reformed Chapel, Broad Chalke, SP5 5EN, GR SU038256

DISTANCE 7½ miles (12km)

SUMMARY Moderate

MAPS OS Landranger 184 Salisbury & The Plain; OS Explorer 130 Salisbury & Stonehenge

WHERE TO EAT AND DRINK The Queens Head, Broad Chalke, T01722-780344; The White Hart, Bishopstone, T01722-780244 (traditional pub food, closed Mon)

A combination of valley and downland in a very pretty part of the country.

START Set off eastwards from the chapel (which now houses the award-winning village stores, open Mon–Sat) and turn left just past the telephone box up the footpath along the side of the churchyard. Turn right onto a tarmac road that comes to an end in a cottage garden. The road now becomes a footpath and runs to the left of the cottage, then straight on between hedgerows and through a long glade of trees.

[1] The path eventually drops down to a concrete farm road, where you turn left up the hill. This takes you into a valley and past farm buildings, then climbs gently between fields.

[2] Where the track bends left, with a wood on the right, look out for a footpath heading into the wood and follow it for 100yds to an open field. Cross the field following the line of lone trees, and continue in the same direction into another wood. Just after a small dip, the path joins a metalled track by a farm gate. Follow this to the crossing track at the edge of the wood.

[3] Turn right (if you carry straight on for 20yds to the brow of the hill you will get a fine view to the northwest over the Nadder Valley). Follow the byway for about ½ mile until, at the beginning of a wood, you come to another crossways.

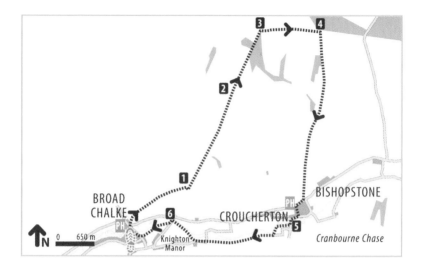

4 Turn right down the hill to Bishopstone. Turn right onto the main road in Bishopstone and then left in front of the White Hart pub. Follow the road through the village, which turns right alongside the River Ebble. The final part of the walk, about 1¾ miles, follows the course of the river back to Broad Chalke. Take the road for Croucheston Mill, cross the river by the fishery and old watercress beds.

5 Almost immediately turn right on a footpath running between streams and over a series of plank bridges. Turn left at the end onto another footpath, then bear right over cattle grids and two stone bridges to reach the mill. Turn right onto a clear path running between hedges and along field edges. This bears left around a house and garden before ending at a gate into the road. Go along the road past Knighton Manor. Immediately you will see a track forking right, which you follow between some large old barns and the water mill (all now converted into houses). Note the old granary on its staddle-stones. The path now keeps to the river, going over a couple of stiles.

6 There is one road to cross: turn left here for 50yds to find the continuation of the path, which runs alongside a big field and comes into the southern end of Broad Chalke close to the church. Turn right down the road to arrive back in the centre of Broad Chalke by The Queens Head inn.

Great Wishford

START The Royal Oak, Great
Wishford, SP2 0PD, GR SU079355

DISTANCE 7½ miles (12km)

SUMMARY Moderate

MAPS OS Landranger 184
Salisbury & The Plain; OS Explorer
130 Salisbury & Stonehenge

WHERE TO EAT AND DRINK The
Royal Oak Inn, Great Wishford,
T01722-790184; The Swan Inn, Stoford,
T01722-790236 (across the river from
Great Wishford; food served all day)

A walk on clear tracks over a hilly area, very much for those who enjoy woodland.

START From the road junction by the inn, proceed under the railway and follow the metalled Grovely Rd, initially in open country, eventually entering Grovely Wood. The road rises steadily, then levels out, until it reaches a junction within sight of Grovely Lodge among the trees, where the track ahead is signed as a 'No Through Road'.

1 Turn right here through a one-bar gate and follow the straight track, on the line of a Roman road, for ½ mile. Through the woodland to the left, a large open area is apparent.

2 On reaching the end of this open area, turn left on a waymarked footpath and, shortly, left again at a junction of tracks (by another waymark). In ½ mile, note a pair of derelict cottages on the right and carry on past Grovely Farm, keeping to the right-hand track at the very edge of the wood.

3 In 400yds, just before the end of the open field on the right, turn sharp left, followed by a sharp right turn 150yds further on. The track emerges from the wood and descends to a one-bar gate as it joins the Ox Drove.

4 An old milestone on the left marks a left turn. Ascend steadily back towards the woodland and follow the track straight on through the trees.

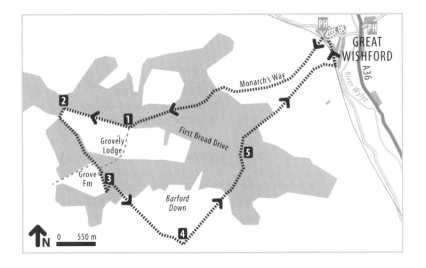

5️⃣ This pleasantly undulating route crosses the trackway on the line of the Roman road, then continues through the woodland before emerging onto open hillside, with long and wide views over the Wylye Valley during the descent to Great Wishford. Pass under the railway and turn left to return to the centre of the village.

Points of interest

 Grovely Wood is an ancient wood, where the villagers of Great Wishford still assert their right to gather firewood in traditional celebrations on Oak Apple Day (29 May).

Great Wishford is a well-situated village off the busy A36 road. The church was substantially restored in 1863–64. Other interesting buildings include the Grobham almshouses (1628) and the Howe school.

Purton & Ringsbury Camp

START Purton church, SN5
4EB, GR SU095871

DISTANCE 7½ miles (12km)

SUMMARY Moderate

MAPS OS Landranger 173
Swindon & Devizes; OS Explorer
169 Cirencester & Swindon

WHERE TO EAT AND DRINK The
Angel Hotel, Purton, T01793-770248

A varied walk through pasture and woodland. Fields and paths are very muddy after rain.

⓵ Walk away from Purton church towards the T-junction, passing the beautiful manor house and barn. Cross the road and take the cycle track opposite, bearing left immediately through a gate. Cross the field towards the cluster of houses to the right of the school to a gate in the opposite hedge. Turn immediately left on a path and bear right towards the stile and gap in the middle of the opposite hedge. Cross this and bear right on a faint path across a field to a kissing gate in the right-hand hedge. Keeping ahead with the hedge on your left, continue through several fields to reach a road. Turn left into the busy road, then, at the next turning on the right, cross the road and take the grassy track to the left of the manor house tennis courts. Turn left past a shed and follow the line of the hedge until you reach a gate near Ringsbury Camp.

⓶ Turn left and shortly cross a stile on the right, following the outside of the fortifications all the way to the gate at the far end. Continue across the field beyond, staying parallel with the left-hand hedge. The path is not easy to follow here: go down the bank beneath a large oak tree and press on until you see a gate ahead. The track beyond leads along the right-hand edge of the wood. At the bottom of the hill a field opens up to the right. Cross this through the gap in the hedge, turn right and then follow the wide, grassy track until you reach a road.

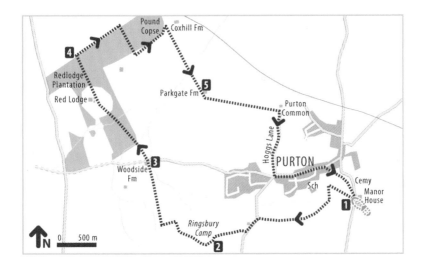

[3] Cross the road and take the track opposite between two cottages and into the wood. After about ¾ mile you reach Hattons Lodge (formerly Red Lodge); look left for a view of the lake. Bear right at the drive of the house to a T-junction. Cross the field opposite to the gate on the other side. Follow a track through trees until you reach the edge of the wood.

[4] Turn right, following the path just inside the trees. Continue to the next track on the right. Follow this to a gate into fields, then turn left along the outside of the wood towards a stile in the next hedge. Now head for the visible gate ahead, keeping fairly close to the edge of the wood. Once inside the copse, turn right and follow the track to a white gate. Continue in the same direction, keeping the hedge on your right.

[5] Walk up the track past the farm, bearing right until you reach a gate. Go through and look for the first, low, double stile in the hedge to your left. Cross the field diagonally to a stile in the hedge and then continue diagonally uphill to a meeting of paths. Go through a gate and take the footpath immediately on your right. Follow this to a double stile. Bear right towards a gate and cross a stile into Hoggs La; follow it to a T-junction. Turn left to walk into Purton, passing on your left two grade II Tudor cottages. Just before The Angel pub take the flight of steps to the right of the pub car park across the road. At the school buildings turn left. At the chapel turn right. Take the first left fork and at the end of the cottages bear right along the path past the cemetery and back to the church.

Aldbourne to Hilldrop

START The Square, Aldbourne
SN8 2DU, GR SU264756
(parking around pond)

DISTANCE 7½ miles (12km)

SUMMARY Moderate

MAPS OS Landranger 174 Newbury
& Wantage; OS Explorer 157
Marlborough & Savernake Forest

WHERE TO EAT AND DRINK
Aldbourne Post Office Café and
Deli, T01672-541353; The Blue
Boar, Aldbourne, T01672-540237

An up-and-down walk partly on quiet roads, but mainly on byways through fields
and woodland.

START Cross the B4192 by the post office and walk along Marlborough
Rd (signposted to Marlborough and Axford). After 100yds leave the main
road as it turns right, and continue along The Butts, past a row of old
thatched cottages. After passing the sports field the road continues uphill
between high hedges, past a junction with two byways, to Ewin's Hill.
Where the hedge ends, there is a good view back to the village and along
the B4192, with Liddington Camp, one of Britain's oldest hill forts, on the
far ridge.

1   At the top of the hill you pass Ewin's Hill Farm on your right.
The lane winds on through a wooded area and emerges on to the
Ramsbury road.

2   Turn right, passing the tree-ringed Laurel Pond. Shortly after this,
turn left along a path signed to Ramsbury. After passing New Buildings,
the path goes on through woodland, with large oaks and cherry trees and
lovely in spring. The track emerges onto the Ramsbury–Marlborough
road, where you turn left. To the left can be seen Ramsbury and its church
and to the right there are glimpses of Ramsbury Manor through the tall
beeches bordering the park.

3   For a better view, walk down the road to the gatehouse; a metalled
road to its left is a right of way that takes you to a bridge overlooking the
lake with the house beyond.

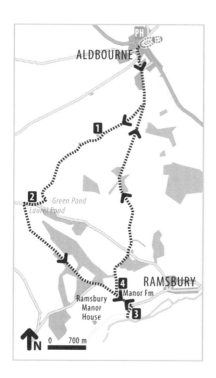

④ Retrace your steps to Manor Farm, where you turn along a bridleway. Shortly you come to a steep ascent beside a belt of woodland. Cross straight over the road at Hilldrop Farm and follow the byway. After a short descent cross another track and begin your last climb, passing a barn on the right. At the top the track veers right by the last stretch of woodland, which is unfenced; on the left are the remains of the wooded Aldbourne Common. To the right of the byway is the site of a Roman building and a distant view of a range of downs, which includes Inkpen Beacon. The last descent gives you a fine view of Aldbourne, the old village and new estates nestling in the folds of the downs, dominated by the church.

Points of interest

Ramsbury Manor is a fine eighteenth-century brick-built house with imposing iron gates.

Lockeridge

START Lockeridge, SN8 4HF, GR SU147679

DISTANCE 7¾ miles (12.5km)

SUMMARY Moderately hilly; woodland section can be muddy

MAPS OS Landranger 173 Swindon & Devizes; OS Explorer 157 Marlborough & Savernake Forest

WHERE TO EAT AND DRINK The Who'd A Thought It, Lockeridge, To1672-861255 (closed Mon)

Part woodland, part downland; easily split into two separate walks.

START From the pub go left along the road. After the last house on the right, bear right by an old fingerpost through a gate and diagonally across a field. Go through a gate and continue across the next field. Through a gateway, a track leads between the River Kennet and a wooded bank. Go through a gate and follow the fence to a stile (beyond which is a sewage works). Turn right along a bridleway under trees. The track comes out onto a road by a cottage. Go left along the road.

1 Shortly, turn right along a bridleway under trees. Pass through a gateway and go straight on into West Woods. At a junction with another bridleway, go right. At a path crossroads, go on, steadily uphill. At the next junction of paths, again go straight on along a bridleway.

2 On reaching a metalled road, go left for 100yds then turn right down a footpath through the woods. This path crosses the Wansdyke (*see* Walks 98/99), a low earth mound and ditch easily recognized by the break in the tree canopy. Cross another track and go straight on. As the route drops to the edge of the woods, a long barrow can be seen among the trees to the right.

3 Join a hardcore track and go left along it. At the road by Bayardo Farm, go right up an unsealed road, leaving the woods behind. Go left around the barn on the left and follow the hedge on the right. Through a gap at the end of the field, turn right along the hedge. In a corner of the field, go through a hunting gate and along the path between fences. Go past a barn on the right, over the brow of a hill and through a gate.

4   At the bottom of the dip, go straight on through two gates. Follow an obvious track across heathland, climbing around the edge of Gopher Wood. Go over a stile into a field and follow the fence, left, at the edge of the wood. Cross a slot stile, across a field to the left end of a line of trees at the edge of the escarpment by a signpost for Knap Hill. Go right along the edge of the escarpment on a grass path by a line of hawthorn. Go over a slot stile by a gate and straight on following the fence, right. The barely discernible summit of Golden Ball Hill is passed (879ft) before you begin descending. Go over a slot stile and straight on, still on the edge of the escarpment, before dropping down to a saddle between a spur of the ridge and Knap Hill. Go through a gate and cross the saddle to see the views from Knap Hill. Return to the gate but go through the metal hunting gate beside it and follow the fence line, right. After passing an old gateway, head towards a group of trees around a pond.

5   Cross the stile to the left of the pond and a jump in the fence, then walk down a valley keeping the fence/hedge on the left. As an overgrown track between hedges comes in from the left, go through a wooden gate and continue with the fence on the right. At the end of the field, carry on between the fence and the trees, then along a broad track. Go through a gate under trees, cross a stile and go straight across a field to a gateway by some trees.

6   Go through, then left along a track under trees. Follow the narrow track down the valley.

7   On re-entering the woods, cross the Wansdyke again. Just beyond is a muddy patch that is difficult to avoid. Beyond this go straight on through the valley on a broad path. At a clearing, fork left along a less obvious track that takes you out into an open area with a picnic table. Cross a track at the lowest point of the clearing, then go uphill past a farm gate to enter woods along an obvious track. At an opening in the tree canopy, cross a triangle of sealed roads and continue on a broad avenue. Leave the woods through a gate near farm buildings on the right. Keep the fence on the right and descend. At the far end, go through a farm gate and on down the slope between hedge and fence to reach the road, opposite a field of sarsen stones, at a junction. Take the road signed 'Marlborough' into Lockeridge.

Shorter, alternative routes: This roughly figure-of-eight route is easily divided into two halves by walking between points 4 and 6, which are only a few yards apart. The woodland section would start from Lockeridge, the downland walk from the car park near Knap Hill. To stay entirely within West Woods, turn right at 3 following the edge of the woods and then go along the Wansdyke to rejoin the main route at 7.

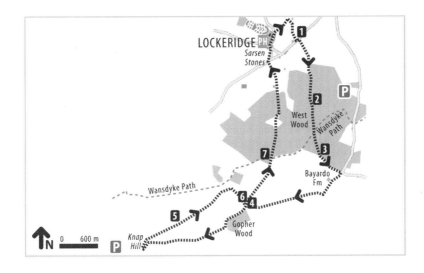

Points of interest

The 856ft Knap Hill was a Neolithic camp, with a commanding position overlooking the Vale of Pewsey. All this ancient landscape has a unique atmosphere through its obvious relics of past civilizations.

On returning to Lockeridge the walk passes a National Trust-owned field liberally sprinkled with sarsen stones, known as 'grey wethers' as they resemble sheep lying in the grass. Sarsen stone was the building material of Megalithic man – dense, heavy and impervious to water, it was formed when silica permeated the sandstone, leaving strange holes where the roots of palm trees once penetrated. Areas of sarsen stone occur naturally all over the downs; to visit a larger field, turn left to Lockeridge Dene, another National Trust reserve.

Upavon & North Newnton

START Market Square, Upavon, SN9 6EA, GR SU134550

DISTANCE 8 miles (13km)

SUMMARY Moderate

MAPS OS Landranger 173 Swindon & Devizes, 184; OS Explorer 130 Salisbury & Stonehenge

WHERE TO EAT AND DRINK The Woodbridge Inn, T01980-630266 (closed Tue, carvery only on Sun; families, dogs and muddy boots welcome); The Ship Inn, Upavon, T01980-630313

A route combining part of the Avon Valley with the open landscape of the Salisbury Plain ridgeway.

START Walk past the Ship Inn and turn left on the main road towards Andover, crossing the Avon. Turn left into Vicarage La (a no-through road). Beyond farm buildings and workshops on the left, go straight on along a rough track. The route at first follows the course of the river then runs alongside the power lines.

1 On reaching a junction of paths, bear left and follow the river again until you reach the main road. Turn left, and cross the river to reach the Woodbridge Inn. Turn right at the telephone box and walk along the road to North Newnton.

2 On reaching a farm, turn left between two large barns and walk through the yard. (North Newnton church can be visited first by a short diversion to the right.) Follow the gently rising track towards Wilsford. As the main track swings to the right, turn left along a smaller track between hedges, signed White Horse Trail. In 50yds the track divides again: take the left fork towards Charlton St Peter. The path, which may be muddy in places, runs between hedges until it joins a farm track leading across a bridge to a metalled road.

3 Go straight ahead, passing a farm, on a track that reaches the main road beside a house that was formerly the Charlton Cat Inn. (Or go left along the road into the village, then down the road beside the church; a footpath beyond the last house on the right crosses a field diagonally to

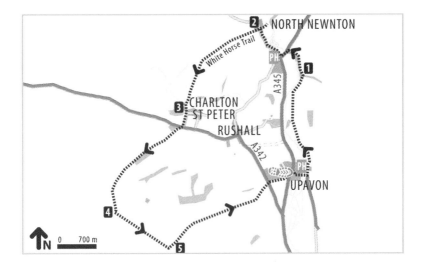

rejoin the route at the main road.) Cross the road and follow a wooded track rising quite steeply. Stay on the stony track, passing a grassy area to the left used as a clay pigeon shoot. You are soon in open country, climbing steadily past the edge of a belt of trees towards the plateau of Salisbury Plain.

④ On meeting the major Ridgeway track turn left, reaching Casterley vedette in ¾ mile.

⑤ Turn left down a metalled road, noting the earthwork of Casterley Camp on the right. Views from this elevated section of roadway include the North Wessex Downs, with the Alton Barnes White Horse (*see* Walk 95) prominent. Cross the main road at the bottom of the hill and go straight on into Upavon.

Points of interest

North Newnton has a simple church near the river, close to a mill. Charlton St Peter church has a Perpendicular tower and chapel, but is otherwise Victorian. This small hamlet was the birthplace of Stephen Duck, the early eighteenth-century 'thresher poet'.

The large, busy village of Upavon has shops, thatched cottages and a church with a thirteenth-century tower.

83

84

85

Hackpen Hill

START Where the Marlborough–
Wootton Bassett road crosses
the Ridgeway at Hackpen
Hill, GR SU129747

DISTANCE 8 miles (13km);
shorter routes 3 miles (5km)
and 6¼ miles (10km)

SUMMARY Easy walking along
obvious tracks, with no stiles

MAPS OS Landranger 173 Swindon
& Devizes; OS Explorer 157
Marlborough & Savernake Forest

WHERE TO EAT AND DRINK If you
do not plan to visit Avebury it would
be wise to carry your own food and/
or drink, especially in extremes of
weather. In Avebury try The Red Lion,
T01672-539266; Circle Café (National
Trust), T01672-539250; there is also a
small post office and general store

A downland walk with magnificent views along the ancient Ridgeway, near
Avebury stone circle.

START Set off left from the car park along the road towards Marlborough,
going southeast and keeping to the grass verge. In about 350yds turn right
down an unsealed track, quite steeply downhill initially, then levelling out.
There are some fine views from here. Where the track meets a tarmac lane
at a T-junction, turn right along the tarmac lane and go over a slight rise.

⓵ Pass through the yard of Wickdown Farm between the house and the
outbuildings. Just beyond the yard, take a grassy track bearing right up
to the brow of the hill, passing just to the right of a small clump of trees.
Follow this track through two gates and go on to where the track is joined
by another coming up from the valley on the left (a conservation area).
On reaching a clump of trees at the top of the hill (with fine views behind
you) follow the track round to the left for a few yards, then turn right
through the trees to a bridleway. Turn right along it to reach a hunting
gate, then cross the field ahead to reach the Ridgeway.

⓶ Turn left along the Ridgeway Long Distance Footpath (*see* Walk 44),
passing a field of sarsen stones and some training gallops on the left. Now
as you gradually lose height, there are extensive views ahead and to the
right. By the gate bearing a sign for the Fyfield Down Nature Reserve, take
the byway off to the right towards Avebury. The track drops down more
quickly now and then levels out.

⓷ Continue down to Manor Farm and take the byway leading to the right through a gate just opposite the first group of buildings. (At this point you may wish to continue past the farm, where the track becomes a road, and on into Avebury to visit the famous stone circle. The track to Winterbourne Monkton is broad and grassy, with a fence on the right, and passes through several gates. A tarmac track is crossed but you continue straight on and over the brow of a gentle rise. Dropping down again to some farm buildings, join a tarmac lane, still going straight on, between hawthorn hedges. At a T-junction in the tarmac lanes, go straight over onto a broad track with a hedge on the left. The path passes a barn on the left and continues ahead on a grassy bridleway. At a track crossroads go straight on; from this point the track can be very muddy in wet weather.

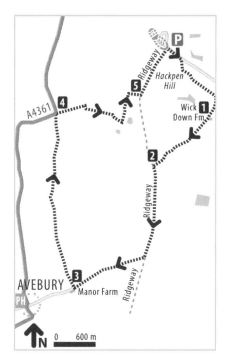

(4) Where the track meets the A361, as the road bends to the left, the route turns to the right along a metalled bridleway. Zigzag to the right and left around farm buildings then continue between a double hedge, back towards the Downs. The double hedge ends at a farm gate on the lower slope of the hill. Follow the track around to the right of the hill, climbing until a gate is reached. Go through and turn left along the top of a field, passing a clump of trees to your right and a small wood to the left. By the gate at the end of the field, go right along a double earth track for a short distance to join the Ridgeway at the next gateway.

(5) Go left along the Ridgeway and follow its broad track all the way back to the car park at Hackpen Hill.

Shorter, alternative routes: Two alternative, shorter walks are arranged by walking either loop of this almost figure-of-eight route. For the 3-mile walk, when you reach the Ridgeway (2), turn right instead of left to return to the car park. For the 6¼-mile walk, from the car park walk south along the Ridgeway and join the main route at point (2).

Dauntsey & Great Somerford

START Glebe Farm, Dauntsey,
SN15 4HR, GR ST981822

DISTANCE 8 miles (13km)

SUMMARY Easy

MAPS OS Landranger 173 Swindon
& Devizes; OS Explorer 156
Chippenham & Bradford-on-Avon

WHERE TO EAT AND DRINK The
New Inn, Upper Seagry, To1249-
721083 (free house, home-cooked
food, closed Mon); The Volunteer Inn,
Great Somerford, To1249 720316

A varied, attractive walk on level ground along good tracks in fields and woods.

START Leave the road by the left-hand farm gate, following the footpath
sign, and walk around the farm buildings, then turn left down the farm
track between hedges. Stay on the track, keeping a hedge on your left, past
another barn and following the field edges, until you reach Dodford Farm.

1 Enter the farmyard and turn right between buildings to continue
through a small car park and straight ahead on a track that follows the
River Avon. The hardcore track peters out into grass along the edge of a
field. Keep the hedgerow on your right and continue, walking under the
power lines, until you reach the weir. Cross the weir to Seagry Mill House.
Turn right and continue up the track between houses for 200yds to a stile
by a gate to the left.

2 Turn left here and walk down to a bridge over a small stream, then
go on to a farm gate. Go straight on along the field edge to another gate,
cross the road and walk down the drive of Manor Farm. Go through
the farmyard, following a series of footpath signs, to reach a stone stile
leading onto another road. Turn right into the village of Upper Seagry,
and continue until you reach a crossroads, with The New Inn on your left.
Turn left at the pub and go down past the houses, looking for a fingerpost
pointing to Lower Stanton on the right at the bottom of the hill.

3 Go through the wooden gate and follow the hedge to a stile by
another wooden gate in the corner. Cross this, turn right for 50yds then
go left along the hedge on your right to the end of the field. Enter Seagry
Wood and almost immediately turn right along the bridleway. Follow it
north to a gate at the end of the woods.

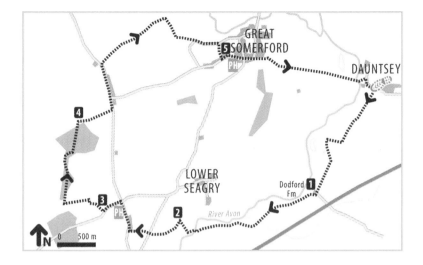

④ Turn right here along a wide grassy track and make for Clove Farm. At the road, turn left and walk through the hamlet of Startley. Opposite Grove Farm turn right down Heath La and go straight on when the road gives way to a bridleway. Turn right at the end on a crossing track and continue until it joins the road. Follow the road as it winds round to the left into Great Somerford.

⑤ As the road becomes Hollow St, just before you reach the old schoolhouse on the right, turn right on a waymarked footpath along the edge of a paddock. Turn left when it reaches the road and continue through the village, over the crossroads and straight on along Dauntsey Rd until you reach Dauntsey Church Bridge after about 1¼ miles. Pass Dauntsey Park House and the church on your left, and continue along the road back to the starting point.

Points of interest

Adjacent to the Georgian Dauntsey Park House, the church of St James the Great contains an extremely rare fourteenth-century painted 'Doom Board' above the rood screen, showing the delights of Heaven and the horrors of Hell.

Around Bishops Cannings

START Smallgrain Plantation,
SN10 2LP, GR SU020671
(car park at picnic site)

DISTANCE 8 miles (13km)

SUMMARY Moderate

MAPS OS Landranger 173 Swindon
& Devizes; OS Explorer 157
Marlborough & Savernake Forest

WHERE TO EAT AND DRINK
The Crown Inn, Bishops
Cannings, T01380-860218

A windswept downland walk with fine views, starting along Wansdyke and
descending to the pretty village of Bishops Cannings.

START From the far end of the picnic site go through the exit behind a
bungalow, left. This leads to a sunken track – part of the Wansdyke ditch
(*see* Walk 51) – which goes up to Morgan's Hill Nature Reserve. Halfway
up the hill there is a signboard describing the reserve. Leave the track here
and bear right through the gate onto a bridleway, heading towards the
telecoms masts.

1   At the top a bridleway crosses the Wansdyke path, with a beech
clump, Furze Knoll, right. Keep straight ahead as the path descends the
downs to the A361 about 1 mile ahead. Cross the main road and pass
between a house and farm buildings to a stile. Walk up the Wansdyke,
which climbs the down ahead. Soon another stile is reached.

2   Cross this and turn right into a chalk lane. Descend on this farm
track for just over 1 mile (with fine views), turning left into a metalled lane
at the bottom, until it emerges on the village street at Bourton. Bear right
here and follow the lane for about ½ mile until you reach a crossroads.

3   Turn left here if you wish to visit the fine church of Bishops Cannings
(*see* Walk 51) and the neighbouring Crown Inn. Retrace your steps from
church or inn to the crossroads. Now turn left, signed 'West End', and
follow the village street for about ½ mile to reach the A361. Cross this
busy road to reach a farm lay-by with several gates. Bear right here and
follow the track up the hillside for about 300yds to a copse.

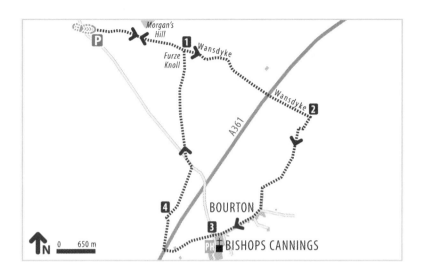

4   Just after the track bends sharply left, there is a gate on the right into the copse. Pass through and follow the path through the trees, emerging into a field at the far end. Walk down the chalk track along the field edge to a road. Cross to the farmyard opposite left and walk through it, then follow the track as it curves up the hill to Furze Knoll, which can be seen again ahead. At the top, beyond the trees 1, turn left along the Wansdyke and walk back to the car park.

Kingston Deverill

START Kingston Deverill church,
BA12 7ES, GR ST845370

DISTANCE 8½ miles (14km)

SUMMARY Moderate, no stiles

MAPS OS Landranger 183
Yeovil & Frome; OS Explorer 143
Warminster & Trowbridge

WHERE TO EAT AND DRINK There
are no refreshments available along
the route, but in nearby Longbridge
Deverill is The George, To1985-
840396, a riverside pub (open for
breakfast from 8am, then all day)

A delightful downland walk mainly on field paths and green lanes.

START Leave the church on your right and walk down the road to the
point where it turns right; a driveway leads off to the left and there is a no-
through road opposite. Cross the road and walk up the no-through road
until it ends at two farm gates. Go through the one on the left and turn left
up a grassy track. At the next gate, turn right along a bridleway (signed
Mid Wilts Way) that rises steadily along the side of the hill, alongside a
fence until it veers away to the left. Continue to walk straight ahead on a
well-defined path, passing a tumulus and a plantation of trees, until a gate
is reached. Go through this gate and straight on until you come alongside
another fence on your left enclosing another plantation. Follow this fence
for a little over ½ mile until you reach a crossing fence.

1   Turn left through the gate at this point and follow the fence on your
right along the end of the Gliding Club runway. Turn right through the
gate by the airfield sign and cross the field, bearing slightly left to a pair
of gates by a solitary tree. Go through and continue with a wire fence on
your right until you reach another gate. Beyond this, continue straight
ahead to a gate that leads out onto a broad metalled lane, the old London
to Exeter turnpike. Turn left and walk along the old road to the B3095,
then cross over to reach a further section of the turnpike. Follow this until,
shortly before reaching the A303, a track runs left along a field boundary.

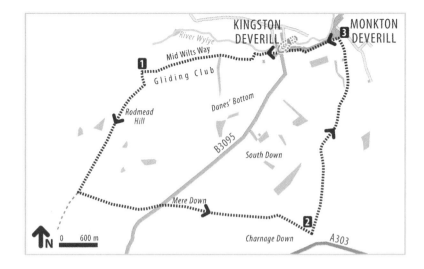

[2] Go along this well-defined path, with the fence on your left, as it rises and falls across the fields to reach a gate at the top of a steep slope. Walk down the path to the floor of a narrow valley. Here, turn left and then right to follow the winding course of the valley until the path ends at a gate by farm buildings.

[3] Go through the gate onto a narrow metalled lane. Follow this down to a T-junction in the village of Monkton Deverill. Turn left and walk a short distance up the road until you come to its junction with the B3095. Turn left and follow the road back into Kingston Deverill and the start.

Points of interest

Much of the walk circles the runway of the Bath Wilts & North Dorset Gliding Club (The Park Gliding Club) on the hill above Kingston Deverill, in use every weekend and bank holiday.

89 Devizes, Seend & Poulshot

START Devizes Wharf Centre car park, SN10 1EB, GR SU004617

DISTANCE 8½ miles (13.5km)

SUMMARY Easy walk on clear tracks

MAPS OS Landranger 173 Swindon & Devizes; OS Explorer 130 Salisbury & Stonehenge, 156 Chippenham & Bradford-on-Avon, 157 Marlborough & Savernake Forest

WHERE TO EAT AND DRINK
The Three Magpies, Sells Green, T01380-828389; The Raven Inn, Poulshot, T01380-828271 (closed Mon); Devizes: any number of inns and restaurants, particularly famous is the Bear Hotel, once home of the painter Thomas Lawrence

This walk includes the most spectacular section of the Kennet and Avon Canal.

START On leaving the car park, cross the canal (*see* Walk 21) by the obvious road bridge to reach the towpath. Proceed in a westerly direction to reach the top lock and main road. The canal is crossed at the Nursery. Carry on, admiring the long views over the Avon Valley, as the canal descends steeply. At the last lock (number 22) cross to the right-hand side of the canal, just before reaching the marina.

① Go under a main road bridge and leave the canal by the next road, heading south towards Seend. On reaching the main Trowbridge to Devizes road turn left to reach Inmarsh La.

② Proceed through Turner's farmyard. Look out for a stile to the right of the farm gate signed 'RHW Engineering'. Cross this and aim to the right of the group of fir trees to reach another stile at the far end of the field. The path continues downhill in a straight line, through a gap between two farm gates, over two more stiles and through another gap, to reach a footbridge in the right-hand corner of the next field

③ After crossing Summerham Brook, keep to the right and climb to a gate. Turn left and follow the bridleway, turning left along the wide crossing track just before reaching Poulshot. At the road, turn right past the Raven Inn. Cross the main road and follow Hay La, a broad track that runs very straight for just over ½ mile. As the track bends sharply to the right, go straight on to cross a footbridge, then cross the field,

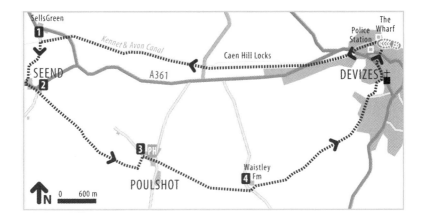

veering towards the hedge on the right. Whistley Farm is ahead. Cross a footbridge and stile in the hedge and continue across the next field to emerge on Whistley Road via a farm gate.

4 Cross the road and follow a track between the bungalow and the near side of the farm buildings. The track rises gradually, with occasional views of Potterne to the right. Beyond Furzehill Farm, Devizes is reached through a wooded cutting, the road by now having become metalled. Follow Hartmoor Rd, cross Hillworth Rd and bear right along a tarmac footpath that skirts the castle grounds. A footbridge over the dismantled railway line takes you to St John's Church. Go left through ornamental gates into St John's Ct, pass the Town Hall and reach Market Sq by St John's St. The Wharf car park can be reached by crossing the square and following Snuff Street and Couch La.

Points of interest

The hilltop village of Seend is the rather unlikely site of a long defunct iron ore extraction industry and once a busy home-weaving centre of Flemish origin. There's a good parish church.

Devizes is a busy market town with an excellent small museum, more than 500 listed buildings, and a particularly well-preserved market place (market day Thu).

90 Around Ashton Keynes

START Ashton Keynes (northwest corner), SN6 6PB, GR SU045942

DISTANCE 9 miles (14.5km)

SUMMARY Easy walk on generally well-maintained footpaths

MAPS OS Landrangers 163 Cheltenham & Cirencester, 173 Swindon & Devizes Swindon & Devizes; OS Explorer 169 Cirencester & Swindon

WHERE TO EAT AND DRINK
The Bakers Arms, Somerford Keynes, T01285-861298 (open daily from noon)

A level walk beside quiet streams and lakes in woodland and meadows rich in unusual flora and fauna.

START Set off along Church Walk and, should you wish to visit Ashton Keynes church, cross the stream (which is, in fact, the Thames) and follow the avenue of horse chestnut trees. Otherwise keep to the left side of the stream, following the footpath as it leads beyond the houses. Cross over a road and continue in the same direction. Follow the Thames Path, with old gravel workings – now lakes forming part of the Cotswold Water Park – on left and right, and continue until the path turns right over the stream. Turn left along the track, later metalled with houses on the left, to reach a road. Cross over and take the footpath opposite to reach a road into Somerford Keynes, bearing right at the first T-junction. The Baker's Arms pub is on the left, about ½ mile further on. About 100yds beyond the pub, turn left down a gravel drive signposted 'Somerford Keynes House Back Gate Entrance'. When you reach the gates, turn right on a footpath that leads to Somerford Keynes church.

1 From the corner of the churchyard follow the signed footpath across the field, with views of the beautiful old manor house behind the church. Cross the footbridge and bear right across the next field to a gate in the opposite hedge, where you turn right, rejoining the Thames Path. Cross the bridge about 100yds beyond Old Mill Farm and turn sharp left away from the river, then right down the farm drive. At the crossroads continue straight on down the lane. Turn left at the grass triangle in Poole Keynes and follow the lane.

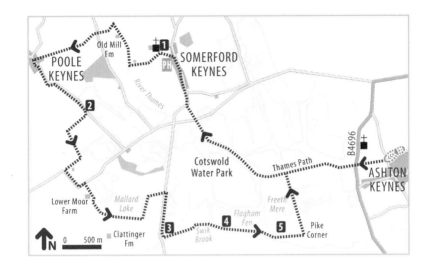

② After passing under the power lines, take a footpath on the right which at first runs parallel with the road, then turns right by a signpost reading 'Oaksey Moor ½ mile'. Go through a gap in the hedge ahead and turn left at the tree-lined brook. Cross the brook by a stone bridge just before a gap in the hedge and walk on towards the buildings ahead of you. Go through the hedgerow to walk around the houses, then through the gate to the left to reach the road. Turn left and follow the road around a corner, then take the signed turning on the right towards Lower Moor Farm. Continue past the car park, visitor centre and barns, and turn left down the track, then take the footpath between the house and farm drives, which is signposted 'Ashton Keynes 2½ miles'. The path runs between hedgerows around two sides of Mallard Lake, then bears right across a field to the road. Cross over and follow the footpath going right between a lake and the road.

③ Turn left through a gate along an avenue of lime trees to join the Swill Brook. The path now runs beside the brook, skirting a series of lakes and meadows that have been carefully managed for wildlife, including beavers and otters.

4 Between Flagham Fen and Freeth Mere 5 the mown paths through the meadows may be easier to negotiate than the overgrown path by the brook. After crossing over a wide wooden bridge and then walking across a large square meadow, turn left at Pike Corner and follow a line of willow trees. At the far end of the lake on your left, go over a stile to rejoin the Thames Path and turn right to return to the start.

Points of interest

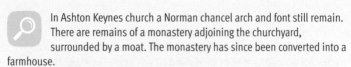

In Ashton Keynes church a Norman chancel arch and font still remain. There are remains of a monastery adjoining the churchyard, surrounded by a moat. The monastery has since been converted into a farmhouse.

Cotswold Water Park provides an interesting example of a landscape in transition. After it was discovered to be a valuable source of gravel, the farmland was quarried away and a number of deep pits formed. When quarrying ceased these were flooded and are now used for watersports, fishing and as nature reserves.

The original Somerford Keynes church dates from 700, though most of what we see is thirteenth century. The small narrow doorway opposite the main entrance is Saxon.

Lower Moor Farm is the gateway to three neighbouring nature reserves comprising lakes, woodlands, wetland and meadows. Clattinger Farm is of international importance for its traditional hay meadow wildflowers, including snakeshead fritillaries and several species of orchid.

Barbury Castle

START Barbury Castle
Country Park, SN4 0QH, GR
SU156780 (large car park)

DISTANCE 9½ miles (15.5km)

SUMMARY Moderate, with
good level footing

MAPS OS Landranger 173 Swindon
& Devizes; OS Explorer 157
Marlborough & Savernake Forest

WHERE TO EAT AND DRINK
Silks on the Downs, Ogbourne St
Andrew, To1672-841229 (no dogs,
no boots); there is usually an ice
cream van at Barbury Castle at
weekends; owing to the exposed
nature of the majority of this route it
is advisable to carry drinking water
(including some for dogs, as there
are virtually no streams or troughs)
and some food in cold weather

An open downland walk, mostly along obvious paths, visiting an impressive hill
fort and two picturesque villages.

START After looking at the extensive views over Swindon and beyond,
walk to Barbury Castle itself, an Iron Age hill fort earthworks (but do
not expect stone ramparts!). From the hunting gate beyond the public
conveniences and information display, cross the level field (pasture) and
go through another hunting gate.

⒈ Either walk through the centre of the fort or along the top of the
perimeter earth walls. Beyond the hill fort go down a fairly steep track
to a last hunting gate onto a tarmac road (there is an information plaque
and signpost here). Turn left along a narrow road, going gently downhill.
From here there are fine views ahead across downs. Where Barbury Castle
Stables' private road goes off to the left follow the track straight on, down a
slight dip by a pond and then up again. Just over the brow of the hill some
training gallops can be seen. Go left here and walk around the edge of the
gallops. Cross a stile and go gently downhill and follow the gallops around
to the right where a double grass and chalk track branches off along the
left side of the gallops. The level track curves around the spurs of the
hillside, which is dotted with horse jumps and obstacles.

2   About 75yds past the corner of a fence running downhill on the left, leave the track and cross the fence (currently by means of a wooden jump, as there is no stile) and bear right up the escarpment along a fairly well-defined grassy path, which gradually rises to the fence visible at the top. Cross the stile and continue in the same direction, heading diagonally across the gallops towards a clump of trees surrounding a barn visible on the skyline. Make for the lower, nearer clump of trees when they come into view.

3   Duck under the fence at the signpost and take the byway curving left around the trees. When you reach the barn, stay on the byway as it curves off to the right (waymarked on the right-hand fence). After about 200yds a hedged enclosure on the left conceals a small cemetery. The track continues downhill, passing barns on the right and under a hangar of mature beech trees, left, all the way into Ogbourne Maizey. At the road go straight along it for 50yds, then take a footpath on the left through a wishing gate. (Dogs may find a welcome drink at the River Og just 50yds beyond the footpath turn-off. Any further upstream is likely to be dry in summer.) The footpath passes through a line of trees. Go through a gate into a field and through another gate on the far side, and straight on towards the church. Cross a farm track (or turn right along it and into the village of Ogbourne St Andrew to find the pub) and pass between houses and gardens, then under a wooden archway into the churchyard. Leave through a gate on the far side and turn right along the road. At a T-junction go left for a short way until the road bends right and there take a double track to the left. The track passes between hedges, crosses a farm track and continues straight on. Where another track goes to the right, keep straight on (both directions are signed 'Ridgeway'), passing between, then under, trees. Go downhill to a road. Go straight ahead, following the signpost to the Ridgeway. About 75yds along the road go left onto a broad concrete, then unsealed track, going slightly uphill and signed 'Ridgeway'.

4   After a slight right bend, bear left through a farm gate, following the Ridgeway path. You go very gradually uphill all the way to Barbury Castle car park, following a well-defined grassy track. Go through Herdswick Farm pastures, then along an unfenced path on the top of Smeathe's Ridge. Note the ancient field systems to the right.

5   Finally, go through a hunting gate onto a broad stony track and turn right, passing Upper Herdswick farm, to return to the car park.

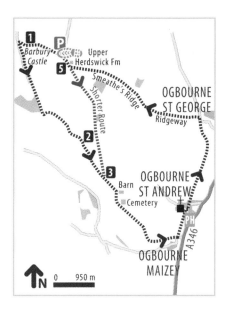

Shorter, alternative routes: To divide the walk into two shorter loops (or for a quick return to the car park) use the broad, stony track between points ③ and ⑤, a stretch of 2 miles (3km).

Points of interest

Barbury Castle is within a Country Park, with a car park, picnic tables, public conveniences, information boards, an ice cream van and marvellous views north. There is frequently hang gliding or kite flying to watch. The highest point of the walk is here, at 879ft (268m).

It was a very different place in the Iron Age. The hill fort, with its three clearly defined circles of ditch and mound, was a refuge for the people and their livestock who came from small settlements around in times of danger.

Barbury Castle and Smeathe's Ridge form part of the Ridgeway Long Distance Path, stretching from Ivinghoe Beacon in the east to Overton Hill on the A4 to the west. For most of the way the path follows the route of the ancient Ridgeway, probably the oldest road in Europe and certainly older than the Iron Age earthworks along it. The section of the path included in this walk is a modern deviation to avoid 4 miles of tarmac near Chiseldon (the ancient route passes below Barbury Castle on the very edge of the escarpment, thence towards Chiseldon and on to Fox Hill).

93

94

Chiseldon

START The Patriots Arms, Chiseldon, SN4 0LU, GR SU184794

DISTANCE 10½ miles (17km)

SUMMARY Easy

MAPS OS Landranger 173 Swindon & Devizes, 174 Newbury & Wantage; OS Explorer 157 Marlborough & Savernake Forest

WHERE TO EAT AND DRINK The Inn with the Well, Ogbourne St George, T01672-841445; The Patriots Arms, Chiseldon, T01793-740331

Easy walking with mostly level ground and gentle gradients.

1 From the front of the pub, go right (east), using pavements, a footpath and wide grassy verges to avoid the traffic. Just past Canney Close, a cul-de-sac on the left, a footpath is well signposted to the right at the edge of a field, following the hedge on the left. At the far end of the field, go through a kissing gate into a lane. Go left along the lane for 200yds. Before the main road (A435), turn right onto a disused railway line.

2 Head south alongside the railway line. The main road is about 50yds to the left, running almost parallel to the path. After almost 1 mile, the path bends left off the railway line to pass between an embankment and the road, going through a clump of Scots pines onto a tarmac lane. Go right, then left, to rejoin the railway line. The route passes between a double hedge of shrubs and trees, a real wildlife haven. Where a bridge once took the railway over a track at right-angles, but is now dismantled, the path descends to the track, on the left of the old bridge, crosses the track (*) and goes up the other side to rejoin the railway. Pass through a very sheltered cutting. Cross a tarmac lane, passing houses on the left with a farm down the lane to the right. Where the railway used to cross a track via a low bridge (now gone), descend to the right onto the track and go along it for 20yds before doubling back to rejoin the railway line by some kennels.

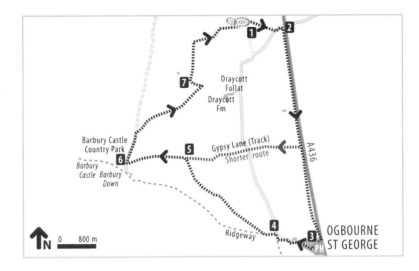

[3] A little further on, almost into Ogbourne St George, go up out of the cutting and onto a concrete track at right-angles to the railway, towards some houses. This metalled lane is Jubb's La. A short way on into the village, at a T-junction, turn right. Follow the road through the village, past a school on the left, to pass a drive to the church on the right (worth a visit if time permits). Where the road goes right and the Ridgeway Long Distance Path is signposted left and right, go right on the road for about 50yds then left (signed for the Ridgeway) onto a broad concrete then unsealed track going slightly uphill. At the brow of the hill and a slight right bend, keep right on the bridleway leading to Smeathe's Ridge.

[4] At first, the path runs between a double hedge, then between a double fence with pasture on the left, up the escarpment to the downs. This section is quite exposed so beware of extremes in the weather. When the fence on the right ends, you join a concrete farm road coming in from the right and continue straight on, past a conifer plantation and pens on the left. There is an earth track from here, with trees forming a hedge on the left. This section can be very muddy but the worst is avoidable.

[5] After ½ mile a double-hedged track comes in from the right (**). Go left along a path signed for Burderop Down. There is a brief section under bushes/trees which can be muddy, but then you are out into the open. There is a signpost where the track divides.

6 Bear left and uphill to Barbury Castle (*see* Walks 91/92). There is a steep but brief climb to a stile by a wire-and-stake gate, then a more gradual climb, with the fence on the left. At the top, pause for breath and to take in the wonderful views. Go over a stile by a farm gate onto a road. Go left for 50yds to reach the Barbury Castle car park, the highest point of the walk at 880ft, where there are further panoramic views. Retrace your steps to the road and go downhill over a stile, through a farm gate and down the hill. After 300yds, pass a track to the left, signed 'Ridgeway, Barbury Castle', and almost immediately take a track on the right along a section of the original Ridgeway. The track is very broad; continue along it for about a mile to the lane to Draycott Farm, and where a footpath crosses the track, go left, leaving the Ridgeway.

7 After 100yds the path divides; go straight ahead for ½ mile until you see a well-formed single path running right, unfenced, across the last field into Chiseldon. Pass behind the first few houses and between the last gardens onto the Draycott road. Go left for 50yds and the Patriots Arms car park is on the right.

Shorter route: For a shorter walk, where the path descends from the railway line to a track at right-angles (*), instead of crossing the track and continuing along the railway route, go right along the track. Cross a road and continue straight on along the double-hedged track, which may be muddy, until a junction of tracks (**) is reached. Now continue as for the main walk.

Pewsey Wharf to Knap Hill

START Pewsey Wharf car park,
SN9 5NT, GR SU158610

DISTANCE 10½ miles (17km)

SUMMARY Moderate, with
some climbs on good paths

MAPS OS Landranger 173 Swindon
& Devizes; OS Explorer 157
Marlborough & Savernake Forest

WHERE TO EAT AND DRINK The
Waterfront, Pewsey Wharf, T01672-
564020 (bar and bistro); The French
Horn, Pewsey Wharf, T01672-562443
(across the bridge from the car
park, closed Tue); The Barge Inn,
Honeystreet, T01672-851705 ('crop
circle pub of the year', every year)

A picturesque stretch of canal and exhilarating downland paths combine to make
a substantial walk.

START Proceed along the canal towpath towards Devizes, passing Stowell
Park and a small suspension bridge.

☐1 In about 2 miles Ladies Bridge is reached. Here the canal looks like
an ornamental lake as it passes through the grounds of Wilcot Manor.
It is believed that Lady Wroughton would agree to sell land to the canal
company only if it was constructed in this manner. This belief remains
unproven! Continue to Honeystreet, with splendid views of Pickled Hill
and Woodborough Hill.

☐2 At Honeystreet the route leaves the canal and follows the metalled
road to Alton Barnes, but don't fail to divert for a short distance further
along the towpath to the Barge Inn, a genuine canalside pub where
refreshment of all kinds is available. Turn right in Alton Barnes following
the sign 'Saxon Church'. Just before reaching the church pass through a
revolving turnstile on the left and take the unusual cobbled path towards
Alton Priors church. Go over two small bridges and through three more
revolving stiles to reach the metalled lane in Alton Priors. Follow this lane
to the Devizes–Pewsey road. Turn left, then almost immediately right into
a minor road – from which the Ridgeway (see Walk 44) branches off to
the right, climbing between trees towards the crest of the Downs. (If this
path is overgrown, a parallel permissive path runs along the edge of the
field to its right.) On reaching a metalled road, turn left and walk downhill
for 300yds.

③ Turn sharply right onto a well-defined chalky path, rising steeply from the road. The Pewsey Downs National Nature Reserve is shortly entered and a good path passes close to the long barrow known as Adam's Grave. The Alton White Horse is an optional diversion to the left, and the views over the Pewsey Vale are extensive.

④ On reaching the grassy path that runs from the White Horse, turn right along it to reach the road, joining it at a small car park. Walk through the car park onto a wide track known as Workway Drove. Turn left through a gate with a noticeboard beside it and make for the crest of Knap Hill up the right-hand path (or skirt it by taking the lower path to the left). On the other side of the hill go over a stile by a gate and follow the right-hand path up the next hill. Continue along the edge of the Downs for a further mile, following the line of squeeze stiles.

⑤ Just before reaching Gopher Wood, turn right by a signpost and descend by a track that skirts the wood then descends steeply to reach a metalled road a little to the north of Draycot Farm. Proceed past the farm, go straight across a crossroads and take the second turning to the right, following the cycleway sign, to reach the canal. Turn left along the towpath to return to Pewsey Wharf in just under 1 mile.

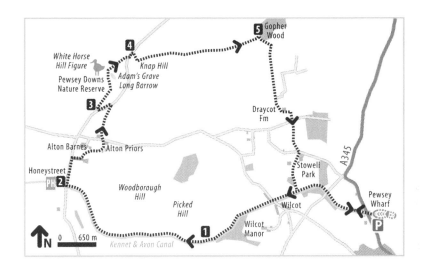

Points of interest

Alton Barnes and Alton Priors are small hamlets with churches remarkably close together. St Mary's, Alton Barnes, shows evidence of its Saxon origins and has a Georgian gallery. Alton Priors church is old and simple and has escaped major Victorian restoration.

The Alton White Horse was cut in 1812 at the expense of Robert Pile, a local farmer. It is about 1,675ft long and 160ft high.

96

97

Aldbourne

START The Square, Aldbourne, SN8 2DU, GR SU264756

DISTANCE 11½ miles (19km) or 9 miles (14.5km)

SUMMARY Moderate walk on clear tracks

MAPS OS Landranger 174 Newbury & Wantage; OS Explorer 157 Marlborough & Savernake Forest

WHERE TO EAT AND DRINK
Unless you carry your own food and drink, the only opportunity for any refreshments is in Aldbourne, which has pubs, a café/deli (in the post office) and a small supermarket; The Crown, To1672-540214 (serves food all day); The Blue Boar, To1672-540237 (on the village green; very old, small and quaint)

A circular route on high downland with extensive views over the rolling countryside.

START From the pond, walk up The Green, to the right of Smithfield House, passing the village green and the Blue Boar pub. Take the road to the right of the church, going slightly uphill, past houses to the right near Crooked Corner. About 100yds further on take the broad, hardcore track forking left, signed as a bridleway, which goes slightly uphill under trees. The track rises gradually, leaving the trees behind to give views all around, and beyond the brow of the hill it undulates gently. After a farm gate it winds between the first and second of four Neolithic burial mounds – the Four Barrows. Pass a small wood on the right, after which the M4 can be seen (and faintly heard) away to the right across the side of the hill. The route climbs gently to the brow of Sugar Hill, with a wood on the right with extensive views in all other directions.

① At a junction with a byway where the woods end, go left, then turn right by a farm gate, signed to Liddington Castle, and follow the fence left along a broad, grassy track. The route is clear all the way, rising very slightly again before dropping down. Where a bridleway leads to the right, go straight on and climb gently uphill again. To the right, you can see the mast on the top of Fox Hill. Keep to the fence on the left, ultimately walking alongside the road, but staying in the field.

② At the top of the rise, just before the road reaches Liddington crossroads, cross the road by a signpost and go straight ahead on a hardcore track. This runs uphill, climbing a little more steeply. Look back to the left to see a view of the route so far.

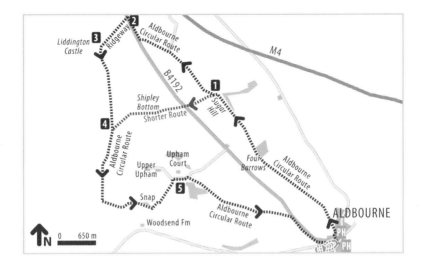

[3] At the top the path bends round to the left, and Liddington Castle can be seen ahead. To visit the castle, go right along the permissive path. Go through a kissing gate then left along the fence line until you reach the earth ramparts of this excellent example of an Iron Age hill fort. The fort is halfway around the walk and also its highest point. From it, the views are superb. Return to the track [3] and continue along it, joining a hawthorn hedge along the flat top of the hill. The route drops gradually down as it runs along the field edges. Continue past a footpath on the right signed to Chiseldon, and another track that comes in from the left signed 'Aldbourne Circular Route shortcut'.

[4] Here, join the Ridgeway byway, continuing in the same direction. At a T-junction of tracks, go right then almost immediately left. There are fine views to the right when the track passes under trees. At an obvious crossroads of tracks, with a mast visible to the right, go left along a hardcore track. After about 300yds, where the track turns right, go straight on through a gate and down a small valley across pasture. When you reach the woods on the right-hand side, go through the farm gate and straight on along the byway under the trees. This is the site of the abandoned hamlet of Snap. Another track comes in almost immediately from the right. Continue along this, passing a signpost to Woodsend to the right. It may be muddy under the trees. Follow the track left and downhill, crossing the valley, then right for 50yds.

(5) Turn left uphill on an unsigned but clearly defined bridleway diagonally across the field, then left again when you reach the track at the top. It ends at the road for Upper Upham. Turn right, and after a short distance, look left for a view of Upham House, a beautiful Tudor mansion built in 1599. About 50yds after the road bends left, go through a farm gate on the right by a byway sign, and along a broad, grassy path between fences. Go through another gate and then straight on across an open field to the next gate with a copse of trees beyond. The broad, double grassy track passes over a slight rise with the copse on the left. Go through open fields with views ahead. Dropping down the spur of the hill, pass tumuli and a wood on the left, with another tumulus, Giant's Grave, among the trees. Continue down to the main road, where you turn right to return to the village and the starting point.

Alternative route: For the shorter version, go straight on at (1) down the hill to Shipley Bottom, crossing the B4192, and follow the byway up the hill to join the Ridgeway at point (4).

Points of interest

Little remains of the hamlet of Snap now, only heaps of stones among the trees. The forty to fifty inhabitants gradually left as the demand for agricultural workers declined in the later nineteenth century, and the two farms here were turned into a sheep run. The last person to live in Snap died in 1910. The name suggests it was once a Viking settlement, but it does not figure in the *Oxford Dictionary of English Place-Names* because it had already ceased to exist when the dictionary was first published in 1936.

The route from Liddington Castle to the turn-off for Snap is along the Ridgeway Long Distance Path, which stretches from Ivinghoe Beacon in the east to Avebury in the west. However, the ancient route of the Ridgeway passes to the north of Liddington Castle and on directly west. This diversion was created by the Countryside Commission to cut out nearly 4 miles of tarmac along the true Ridgeway, and in doing so added in some of the most beautiful stretches of the Marlborough Downs.

Bishops Cannings & Wansdyke

START Crossroads in Bishops Cannings, just off the A361, SN10 2LD, GR SU036643 (car park at crossroads)

MAPS OS Landranger 173 Swindon & Devizes; OS Explorer 157 Marlborough & Savernake Forest

DISTANCE 12 miles (19km) or 14½ miles (23km)

SUMMARY Easy first section (towpath muddy in wet weather); more challenging hill walking

WHERE TO EAT AND DRINK The Crown Inn, Bishops Cannings, T01380-860218 (traditional pub food); The Kings Arms Inn, All Cannings, T01380-860328 (frequently changing menu, open fires, dogs welcome, closed Mon lunchtimes)

A gentle canalside walk through the Vale of Pewsey followed by an exhilarating return along the crest of Wansdyke.

START Walk down the road signposted to Horton to reach Bishops Cannings church and pub. Go through the churchyard and between houses on Church Walk, then turn right into the road. Where the road bends right to go to Court Farm, go straight ahead on a footpath along a farm road, through the touring-caravan site and across a swingbridge over the Kennet and Avon Canal, then along a grassy track between hedges. Another footpath goes off right but you keep straight on. The path opens out and goes across a field towards a farm. Go through a gate at the corner of the fence and around a paddock and barn, then turn right on Horton Mill Farm drive to join a road. Go left through Horton village. Before the bridge over the canal, turn right along the grassy towpath. Pass the disused swingbridge, go under the next bridge and pass a dismantled bridge and foot swingbridge.

[1] Turn right here across the field if you wish to visit the pretty village of All Cannings and the Kings Arms Inn, returning up the village street and turning right on a byway signposted to Patney Rd, then left to reach the brick bridge. Alternatively, continue along the towpath to the bridge, and cross the canal. About 50yds beyond the bridge, turn right through an opening and follow the path around the edge of the fields, at first parallel to the canal but then veering away left around a series of paddocks. Go right along a tarmac road. The road bends left by Pewsey Vale Riding Centre and then on through Stanton St Bernard village. Pass a cul-de-sac on the left and take the next turning left. The road bends sharp left after 75yds. At the main road, go right for 100yds then cross the road

and follow a signed footpath left heading for Milk Hill. After crossing an unsurfaced farm track with buildings to the right, go through the gate at the foot of the hill into Pewsey Down National Nature Reserve. Go left, keeping parallel to the fence on the left but slightly above it, around the hillside along narrow, grassy sheep-tracks. In the corner of the field, without passing through the gate, turn right up the fenceline. Keeping the fence left, climb steeply up the hill towards a tree plantation.

2 When you reach the trees, a gate to the left leads to a path around the top of a steep valley. Pass a copse on your left to join an unsealed track leading to the Wansdyke 5. Go left and over a stile by a gate to follow the Wansdyke west. For the longer option, turn right instead of left by the trees, and walk around the plantation until you see Alton Barnes White Horse. Go straight on to reach it, with spectacular views over the Vale of Pewsey. Keep above the White Horse and follow the obvious, narrow path on across the slope to the hill beyond. Around the spur of the hill, Adam's Grave is visible on the next rise. The path drops down, crosses a small ditch/mound and rises again to visit the long barrow.

3 After admiring the views from the long barrow, return to the ditch/mound and go right through two gates to reach a road by a small car park.

4 Go through the gate opposite the car park. Now, either (for keen archaeologists) go diagonally right along the ancient Ridgeway, first across a field to pass between a wood and farm, then along a well-defined track gradually uphill to reach the Wansdyke under the trees. Go left along the Wansdyke, following the track on its south side. Or, follow the bridleway from the road, passing a wood on the right and following the fence on the left to the top of the rise. Cross the Wansdyke through a gap in the mound, then turn left and over a stile by a gate. The route west stays along the Wansdyke, mainly along the top of the mound, with occasional stiles to cross fences, but is always clear.

5 At an unsealed farm road (where the extension rejoins the shorter route) the Wansdyke begins climbing gradually and bends to the right, passing below the summit of Tan Hill (equal in height to Milk Hill). At a gate the path diverts to the right of the Wansdyke along a track. Turn left down Manor Farm bridleway to return to the path on top of the mound. Cross the muddy track (leading to a water tower visible on the left) with a stile and gate either side.

6 At a hardcore track, turn left, over the brow of a slight rise and past a group of farm buildings on the right. Go gently downhill with the spire of Bishops Cannings church visible ahead. Pass through the yard of Easton

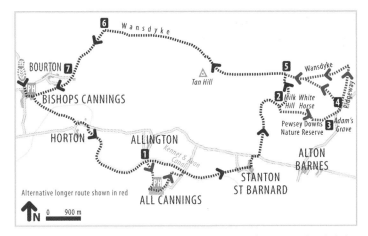

Farm and beyond the house turn right onto a road, then immediately left through a gate onto a path signposted to Bourton and Bishops Cannings.

7️⃣ Go across the paddocks following the route indicated, eventually with a hedge on your left. Cross a footbridge under trees into the next field, then go over another footbridge and continue along the edge of a field, past buildings and paddocks. Reaching a thatched cottage, head across the field towards the village. Go over a footbridge and stile, then turn right along the edge of a field, towards the steeple. At the corner go through a narrow gate into a lane. Turn left to reach a road, cross it and go straight on along Church Walk, then retrace your steps to the car park.

Points of interest

Bishops Cannings, *see* Walk 51.

Pewsey Downs National Nature Reserve contains a landscape that is unspoiled, natural downland, never having been under the plough. Threatened species of native flowers and butterflies thrive in the protected environment.

A broad, flat, very exposed hill, Milk Hill is the highest in Wiltshire at 964ft.

The Wansdyke dates from the sixth or seventh century. This huge earthwork was built by the ancient Britons as a defence against Saxons invading from the North. It was clearly successful, as no pagan Saxon burials have been found south of here. The point where the Ridgeway – older than the Wansdyke and Adam's Grave, and probably the oldest road in Europe – crosses the Wansdyke was once an important place: the main trading route of the time crossing the frontier between two kingdoms.

100 Around Sutton Veny

START Sutton Veny church, BA12 7AP, GR ST902417 (car park by primary school)

DISTANCE 12 miles (19km)

SUMMARY Moderate walk, mainly on stony tracks

MAPS OS Landrangers 183 Yeovil & Frome, 184 Salisbury & The Plain; OS Explorer 143 Warminster & Trowbridge

WHERE TO EAT AND DRINK The Woolpack, Sutton Veny, T01985-840834 (closed Mon)

A walk along ancient trackways over high, remote chalk downlands.

START Turn right out of the car park. At a crossroads turn left into Hill Rd and follow it up onto the downs, joining another road coming up from the left. After passing Haycombe Hill Farm, left, the road bears round to the left beside a barn, where it ends. Continue along a broad, well-defined track, passing a clump of beech trees. At a crossing byway, turn right and go down towards the A350.

1 Just before you reach the main road, turn left along another byway between tall hedges.

2 At the apex of Botley Oak Brake another track merges from the left (for a shorter walk, omitting the section to Higher Pertwood, turn left here). Continue over the brow of the hill to pass a derelict Dutch barn, then go straight on down the hill and up through Bockerly Coppice, following the bridleway sign by a farm gate at the top of the rise.

3 Just after it emerges from a double hedgerow, turn sharp right on a footpath up the field edge. About 50yds before reaching the belt of trees at the top look for a wooden gate on the right and go through the trees to emerge in a field. Follow the right-hand edge to a gate in the lower corner, then go left across the top of the next field and descend to a farm gate. Continue up the track into Higher Pertwood. Passing between two small, neat greens, bear right in front of the Manor House, then turn left between two brick gateposts and walk towards a barn. To its left is a path leading to the church of St Peter, restored in the 1990s. Retrace your steps through the hamlet and take the farm track leading off to the left to return

to the byway near the old Dutch barn. Turn left and walk back towards Botley Oak Brake. Just past a bridleway sign take the unmarked track through a hedge gap to the right ② and continue with the hedge on your left. Ignore a byway going off left through Little Sutton Woods, and continue along the track to the right of the wood.

④ When it starts to bend to the right, go straight on through a farm gate and downhill to join a broad chalk track. Follow this down through Redding Hanging to the bottom of a steep valley. Pass through a gate and follow the track up out of the valley, passing through another gate by a Dutch barn at the top of the hill, where a track merges from the left. Continue to follow the track to the point where it turns sharply left in front of a gate and farm buildings. Follow it around and continue to the Wylye Valley road at the western end of Tytherington.

⑤ Turn right and walk a short distance down the road to visit the church of St James. Retrace your steps up the road and take the footpath across the paddock just beyond the houses on the right. Go through a kissing gate under the trees and turn right along the stream (signposted to Sutton Veny). Through another kissing gate, the path runs straight across the fields to the partly ruined church of St Leonard in Sutton Veny. Leave the churchyard at its western end and follow the path down to a road; turn left and walk down to the High St, where you turn right to return to the car park.

Points of interest

The present Manor House stands in the tiny hamlet of Higher Pertwood on the site of a former farmhouse built well before the Norman Conquest. It was built in the eighteenth century, but has been extensively altered. St Peter's church was also built during the eighteenth century but a church has existed on this site since 1332. St Peter's was declared redundant in 1972 and fell into ruin, but was restored and reopened in 1998.

St James's church, Tytherington, is a tiny chapel dating from the early twelfth century, and reputed to be the oldest church in Wiltshire.

St Leonard's church, Sutton Veny, a partially ruined thirteenth-century church abandoned in the 1860s, is now maintained by the Churches Conservation Trust.

Forthcoming titles in the 100 Walks series

- Derbyshire
- Cheshire
- Northumberland
- Surrey
- Staffordshire
- County Durham

Other titles in the 100 Walks series

- Lancashire
- Yorkshire